Celebrating City Teachers

Celebrating City Teachers

How to Make a Difference in Urban Schools

Jill Sunday Bartoli

Foreword by William C. Ayers

HEINEMANN
Portsmouth, NH

Heinemann
A division of Reed Elsevier Inc.
361 Hanover Street
Portsmouth, NH 03801–3912
www.heinemann.com

LC5131
.B37
2001
046575249

Offices and agents throughout the world

The author and publisher wish to thank those who have generously given permission to reprint borrowed material:

Figures 7–1A and 7–1B reprinted from *Grace at the Table: Ending Hunger in God's World* by David Beckman and Arthur Simon. Copyright © 1999 by Bread for the World. Published by Paulist Press with statistical information courtesy of the Luxembourg Income Study. Used by permission of Bread for the World.

Library of Congress Cataloging-in-Publication Data
Bartoli, Jill.
    Celebrating city teachers : how to make a difference in urban schools /
by Jill Sunday Bartoli in collaboration with colleagues in Philadelphia,
Lancaster, and New York City.
      p. cm.
    Includes bibliographical references and index.
    ISBN 0-325-00379-3 (pbk. : alk. paper)
    1. Education, Urban—United States. 2. Elementary schools—
Pennsylvania—Philadelphia—Case studies. I. Title.

LC5131 .B37 2001
372.9748'11—dc21   2001024368

Editor: Lois Bridges
Production: Lynne Reed
Cover Design: Karen Webb
Manufacturing: Steve Bernier

Printed in the United States of America on acid-free paper
05   04   03   02   01   DA   1   2   3   4   5

This book is dedicated to the city teachers, community organizers,
and other urban warriors who are working at the front lines
in support of equal educational opportunity for all children
and of universal human rights.

Contents

Foreword

It is not news that city public schools are failing large numbers of American children. Dropout and illiteracy rates are high, test scores and grades are low. These things are so oft repeated that they gather onto themselves a powerful aura that vibrates with something we might imagine to be the TRUTH—say "city schools" and watch as a small army of poor kids of color marches from behind the curtain of your consciousness and enacts a well-rehearsed caricature of failure already etched in your mind, a script any one of us could have written.

In *Celebrating City Teachers*, a book with important surprises on almost every page, Jill Sunday Bartoli flips the script and challenges us to rethink the insistent dogma we sometimes call "common sense." She demonstrates that the authoritative, automatic assumptions too many of us pass along about the poor are nothing but received wisdom, stereotypes that float comfortably on thick and sticky clouds of ignorance. She portrays real neighborhoods and actual schools where people engage one another in building communities of hope and support. And most important, she shows us that the unbreakable link we expect to find between poverty and school failure is neither necessary nor God-given; it, too, is a social construction, an American myth.

School failure is predictable, but for reasons that have nothing to do with a "culture of poverty," a "tangle of pathologies," or some devastating character trait that resides exclusively inside a specific class of people. School failure can be mapped alongside the "savage inequalities" so prevalent in our society, a relationship that has to do with policy and political will, not human capacity, real or imagined. The richest country in the world has the distinction of having the highest rates of child poverty by far among industrial nations, as well as the lowest rates of reducing child poverty through government spending. This means, among other things, that the schools that need the most in terms of first-rate facilities, materials, personnel, access, and so on, actually get the least.

Children of the poor are most often denied an education of power and possibility in our country. They are denied an education that honors their humanity and invites their full democratic participation. This means most of all that they are denied the right to question, the right to name their worlds, the right to discover a range of answers to the question, Who in the world am I?

Jill Bartoli shows us city teachers who work against this bleak, oppressive backdrop. These are teachers of hope and courage, teachers who see children and youth not as empty vessels to be filled up but rather as propulsive meaning makers, dynamos of energy who are moving, building, reconstructing in endless journeys to make sense and to become competent. These are teachers who are themselves in motion, working with imagination, generosity, and compassion to nourish and challenge their students to keep right on reaching. There are lessons here for all of us.

William C. Ayers
Distinguished Professor of Education
Senior University Scholar
Director, Center for Youth and Society

Acknowledgments

In 1996, when I first began formulating my major questions about successful city teaching and the research process to answer them, I talked with Gloria Ladson-Billings, Seymour Sarason, JoBeth Allen, Pat Carini, Frederick Erickson, Asa Hilliard, and Michael Apple, all of whom offered valuable suggestions and encouragement. As I began to search for schools to pilot, my conversations with Carol Hirschfeld, Bruce Kanze, Lucy Calkins, Betsy Useem, JoAnn Seaver, and other friends from the Philadelphia Teachers Learning Cooperative were most helpful.

During the 1996–1997 year of on-site research, the colleagueship of two city teachers who live in the community and are parents of children who attended the schools where they teach was invaluable. Teresa Alvarez and Andrietta Sims opened their homes to me, for which I will forever be in their debt. Several other wonderful mentors, friends, and colleagues have read and commented upon multiple drafts of this book, and for that Seymour Sarason, Carol Hirschfeld, and JoBeth Allen will forever be on my list of saints.

Cheri Honkala and her fellow Kensington Welfare Rights Union (KWRU) members helped me to better understand the realities of poverty and homelessness in Philadelphia and the power of grassroots organizing. And, like the members of KWRU, Wanda Davis and Rev. Edward Bailey of the Bethel African Methodist Episcopal Cultural Center in Lancaster, Pennsylvania, have been inspiring models of the power of and possibility for change. The commitment and dedication of these tireless community advocates and organizers continually fuel my passion for social justice.

Over the final year of this book's evolution I have greatly benefited from the suggestions and comments of Bill Ayers, Gerry Coles, and most especially Lois Bridges, whose keen insight and wonderful encouragement were gifts from heaven. The final manuscript owes much to Lois' perceptive ideas and suggestions, and to her gracious mentoring.

Introduction

This is a book written in celebration of city teachers. It is about, by, and for the many excellent, knowledgeable, and committed city teachers whose classrooms, schools, and communities I have had the honor to visit over the past five years. It is their knowledge and experience, their perspectives on successful teaching and learning, and their classroom practices that this book seeks to celebrate and share.

During one full year, 1996 to 1997, I had the good fortune to spend time with city teachers in their elementary schools and communities in Philadelphia and New York City. In the years following we continued to collaborate as friends and colleagues, making it possible for some of my college students to meet and learn from these remarkable women.

City teachers cannot be fully appreciated without an understanding of the school and community contexts within which they teach. In this book, after hearing from four of the teachers themselves, we look at city teachers within the ecology of their elementary schools, which were chosen on the basis of the following three criteria.

1. There are respectful and trusting relationships among students, teachers, families, and administrators.
2. There is ongoing, collegial professional development throughout the school, which is grounded in thoughtful research.
3. The school is "successful" in the eyes of parents, faculty, and students in the school as well as outside educational researchers.

In addition to applying these three criteria, I chose sites that reflected common urban public school conditions in the United States, such as a low-income community and population and a high proportion of African American and Latino students. Public schools with low-income and high student-of-color populations are often assumed to have inferior education and high failure rates. And parent and community relationships with urban schools have frequently been viewed as problematic. So I wanted to go where these assumptions and stereotypes were dispelled—where teaching, learning, and relationship building were happening in spite of the odds.

Defining Successful and Unsuccessful Teaching and Learning

Successful teaching and learning, according to the criteria that I have chosen, is not defined by standardized test scores—we do not have standardized tests that are sensitive enough to measure learning in its fullest and richest context and meaning. Over the past half century, the research on language learning in particular, and higher-level critical and constructivist thinking in general, has yielded a broad definition of human learning that has social, personal, integrative, transformative, and ecological components. Unfortunately, we have not chosen to develop and endorse nationally the kinds of thoughtful, comprehensive, contextually meaningful methods that can evaluate this kind of learning.

Instead, we use only decontextualized standardized tests that assess a narrow range of verbal and linguistic knowledge. And this, in turn, is dependent on the language opportunities experienced by the learner. This high-stakes testing practice ensures continued inequality (Kohn 2000; Swope and Miner 2000), creates new inequalities (McNeil 2000), and reveals the educational illiteracy of our most literate policymakers.

My previous research on unsuccessful learning gave me the basis for the criterion of respectful and trusting relationships. From what I have observed over the past twenty years in sites where children are not achieving, there is often a lack of such relationships, as well as a lack of cooperation and collaboration throughout the ecology of the learner (Bartoli 1986, 1995; Bartoli and Botel 1988). In unsuccessful schools the relationships between the teachers and students, teachers and parents, and teachers and principals often showed a lack of trust, respect, and mutual support. Thus the environment in the classroom and school could not generally be described as collegial, caring, and supportive.

In the unsuccessful schools in which I observed there was also a lack of collaborative faculty inquiry, learning, and growth. New ideas and the quest for continual professional development were either not well supported and orchestrated or not a high priority. And it was rare to find schoolwide agreement on how children could learn more successfully and how teachers and parents could facilitate this.

The Search for Success

Comprehensive and longitudinal research on schooling in the United States by Sarason (1971, 1999), Darling-Hammond (1992), Darling-Hammond and Sykes (1999), Goodlad (1987, 2000), Lieberman and Miller (1992, 1999), McNeil (1986, 2000), Ladson-Billings (1994, 2001) and many other excellent educational researchers points to a number of interconnected problems. These include (1) lack of understanding of the complexity of schools as systems, (2) lack of critical and reflective thinking both in classrooms and in teacher-preparation programs, (3) boring and meaningless classroom activities assessed by multiple-choice and standardized testing, (4) a culture of administrative control and dominance, and (5) the particular disadvantage suffered by students who have not had many and varied opportunities to learn the verbal and linguistic material that is promoted, taught, and tested in traditional U.S. schools.

In typical schools in the United States, students whose parents are not economically, socially, racially, or culturally advantaged are less frequently provided with what they need to catch up with those who are. Thus, their experiences with learning and testing, in the typical narrow range of traditional school activities and goals, are more likely to be unsuccessful. They therefore end up leaving the school more disabled or disadvantaged than when they arrived, with the accompanying stigma of school failure, inadequacy, and incompetence (Rist 1972; Rist and Harrell 1982; Mehan 1980; McDermott 1987; Apple 1996; Allington 1995, 1998; Skirtic 1991; Coles 1987, 1998; Armstrong 1995).

My search was for teachers in sites where this failure cycle was not perpetuated—where the disadvantage was interrupted so that there was meaningful learning for all students, regardless of their previous experiences and opportunities. Gloria Ladson-Billings (1994) identified individual teachers who achieved this, and Mike Rose (1995) found many classrooms across the country in which success was evident. The successful urban school described by Deborah Meier (1995) and the democratic schools described by Michael Apple and James Beane (1995) also spoke to the possibilities for success.

Inspired by these models of urban public school success, I wanted to study schools wherein meaningful learning for all students and teachers was a unified goal, actively pursued by the faculty and staff as they worked collaboratively with parents, students, and the community. Since my own area of teaching is language arts, I chose to focus on literacy learning in urban elementary schools, but I also wanted to better understand what good city teachers do to build a community of support, trust, and mutual respect in their schools and neighborhoods.

City Myths and Stereotypes

There are so many fears, assumptions, myths, and stereotypes about "the inner city" or "the ghetto" or "the barrio" that we forget that families live there—families like our own who want the very best for their children. Stereotypes and myths about cities in general, and city schools in particular, are evident in the most common question that I am asked about my research on successful city teachers and their schools: "Well *are* there any?"

Even when I explain that I had many successful schools to choose from, and that I'm attempting to write a book about just a few of them, people have sarcastically remarked, "I guess that will be the shortest book in history." And it is not just the general public offering this negative response. It is also highly literate academics and policymakers.

Having lived among these rather typical white middle-class assumptions for fifty years, it does not surprise me when friends and colleagues respond with their own fears and assumptions. They may look at me as either naive or crazy when I share some of my personal experiences about living and learning in North Philadelphia and Harlem. Their own fears about city subways, city schools, poor city neighborhoods, and the people who live in them are reinforced in daily small-town conversations, and they are perpetuated regularly in the media.

I have tried to tell my own personal city stories in hopes of dispelling some of their fears. For instance, I have told friends about our family trip to New York City, when our son Patrick was just ten years old. Living in our small town of Carlisle, Pennsylvania, all of his life (where, as I write this, the Ku Klux Klan is preparing to speak on the courthouse steps), Patrick has heard many people speaking of their fears and stereotypes about cities—fears of dangerous Black people, and fears of New York City subways.

To calm his fears, and to allay our own, my husband Jim and I gave Patrick very clear instructions about how to avoid getting lost or left alone without us on the subway platform. "When the subway train door opens," we told him, "move *immediately* inside so we don't lose you." Which he did at 79th Street. The problem was that we did not, and the door closed with Patrick inside.

Frantically, we asked the people standing beside us where this train ended, and someone said it went to 253rd Street. Imagining the horror of not knowing where he might end up, or at which stop he might get off, or how terrified he might be, or what might happen to him along the way, we raced to the ticket booth for help. The attendant suggested that we get on the next subway train, and then get off at the next stop. "Kids are smart," she said. "He will know to get off at the next stop and wait for you."

Right. We stood on the platform in agony waiting for the next train. The people around us must have sensed our terror, because they assured us that, even if Patrick didn't know to get off at the next stop, someone on the train would tell him to get off and wait. They seemed confident that someone would help him, and that it would be okay. Their assurances were only moderately comforting.

So we got on the next train, and there at the next stop was Patrick, standing beside a grandfatherly looking African American man, waiting for us. He told us later that there was a twelve-year-old boy, also African American, who was on the train that he got on, and the boy and his family advised Patrick to get off at the next stop to wait. Then, when he got off, the older man waited with Patrick until we came, so that our son would not be alone and afraid.

Harlem Lessons

But even with experiences such as this, I had much unlearning to do, relative to my own well-learned fears and assumptions. I will be forever indebted to Andrietta Sims for my first lesson in Harlem. Andrietta teaches at Central Park East II Elementary School, and she kindly invited me to stay with her family at their home while I was visiting CPE II and PS 114 in Brooklyn. One warm summer evening she took me for a long walk around her neighborhood, showing me where her family had once lived, their apartment building at 139th Street, Sugar Hill, and some of the historic sites and places in the community.

It was a great walking tour of the community, just twenty blocks above where I was staying that summer at Columbia University's International House. Andrietta is a tall, very attractive woman whose long stride kept me walking at an invigorating pace for miles that evening. Several times along the way back to 120th Street we stopped to talk with people she knew, and I began to see her community as just that—a community.

This helped later in the fall when I came to stay with Andrietta and her two children, Kendall and Kendra. I had to catch three different trains that day in Harrisburg, Philadelphia, and Trenton, and it was late evening by the time I arrived in New York City. I managed to find the right subway train, but I missed my uptown stop, getting off at 145th Street instead of 137th, and I ended up wandering around several blocks in the dark. I couldn't seem to get headed in the right direction, and I was getting tired, weighted down by my heavy backpack and the suitcase I was pulling behind me. I remember feeling very alone, very lost, and for the first time, very afraid.

Then I realized that it was my own fear and stereotypes about Harlem that were keeping me from asking people on the street for help. Finally remembering my earlier summer walking tour with Andrietta, I asked for direction from the next person I saw, who kindly headed me toward 139th Street and the river. And I continued to ask for help at each intersection until I got to Andrietta's apartment building, receiving only kindness and helpfulness from the people I spoke with.

Later I wondered what had created my fears and negative assumptions. I wondered how the myths and stereotypes that fed these assumptions developed. I wondered about the nature of the ecology that has evolved in city schools and communities in the United States in the midst of such assumptions. And I thought about the possibilities for changing the assumptions, the stereotypes, and the lived reality for teachers and students in city schools and communities. This book explores these complex questions, and it offers examples of individuals and communities creating an ecology for successful learning rather than failure.

Learning from City Folks

One morning, on the bus ride to visit Andrietta's school in East Harlem, I watched as young schoolchildren got on the bus and greeted the bus driver; they seemed comfortable riding on the city buses. One little boy sat near the driver and had a long conversation with him, which changed my image of the presumed impersonal nature of city bus drivers. The driver talked with the little boy about eating healthy food, what he liked to cook at home, and what his mom cooked that he really liked. When the little boy got off the bus to go to his school, the driver wished him a good day as the boy smiled and waved happily in reply.

Another lesson was offered when I was leaving the city, a situation that was similar to my arrival. (I have to add here, in self-defense, that for the time that I was there, I got all of the right buses and subway trains.) Instead of getting on the bus that would connect me with the subway train to Penn Station at 34th Street, I got headed uptown on the wrong bus after leaving the school. When I looked out of the window and saw the sign for 158th Street, I had the sense to ask the woman behind me on the bus for help. She, in turn, asked the man behind her, and he talked with the person behind him. In a few short minutes they had a group plan to get me on the right bus and subway train to the 34th Street train station.

I still remember the warm feeling I had, getting off the bus to cross the street and looking back to see half of the people on the bus either pointing me in the right direction or smiling and waving goodbye. So my overall impression and experience of the Harlem community was far different from the media myths. And while it is true that the store across from Andrietta's apartment building is known for dealing drugs, I wasn't bothered by anyone when I stopped in to get some milk and bread.

Both at Andrietta's home and Teresa Alvarez's home in North Philadelphia, there is evidence of a less-than-responsive sidewalk and street-cleaning system at work in the community. But the lovely flowers and well-kept walkways around Andrietta's tenant-owned building belie the "those people don't care" myth. And when Teresa's students see the beautiful interior of the home that she and her husband remodeled themselves, their eyes shine with delight at such loveliness in their own community.

In both of these communities there are also absentee property owners and slumlords whose buildings are left to deteriorate. Neglect (by those who have the money and power to maintain it, as well as their distance from it) is one of the many problems in the larger ecology of city schools and communities. But the sad results in the community from profiteering and distant property owners must not be confused as a reflection of choices made by supposedly neglectful or uncaring members of the community.

Dispelling the Myths

It is simply not true that urban public schools and teachers are to blame for the high rates of failure and "at risk" children and youth in cities across the United States. Nor is it true that the children and families who live in poor urban communities are inherently unfit, deficient, disabled, or hopelessly disadvantaged. Likewise, it is not true that most urban teachers in the United States are incompetent and providing inferior education to their students, compared with teachers from better-funded suburban schools.

Having observed in literally hundreds of suburban and urban classrooms over the past twenty years as both a researcher and a supervisor of interns and student teachers, I believe I have a fair base of comparison. And if I honestly confessed the number of times that I have stood spellbound and in awe of the teaching that I have observed in city schools, or been moved to tears of admiration and deep respect while observing in city classrooms, I would surely be accused of being what my older sons might call "sappy" (roughly translated as overly sentimental).

Cultural assumptions about low-income urban communities, as well as racial and ethnic stereotypes, fuel the negative generalizations about city schools, teachers, families, and communities. And political, social, historic, economic, and corporate practices maintain them. Not enough longitudinal and ecological research has been published on successful city schools, teachers, and communities to counter these negative stereotypes and assumptions, particularly for the general public. And the positive research studies of Taylor and Dorsey-Gaines (1988), Rose (1995), Meire (1995), Ayers and Ford (1996), Apple and Beane (1995), and Ladson-Billings (1994, 2001) have not received the wider public press that they deserve.

Kozol's (2000) *Ordinary Resurrections* addresses some of the myths, but on the whole, stereotypes go unchallenged in the media, feeding the destructive racial and economic biases that have prevented our country's progress toward a more equitable, inclusive, democratic society. And so little has been done to prevent their destructive impact on the education, health, and social welfare of children and families in underresourced urban communities.

Uninformed cultural assumptions and biases strongly affect urban families' opportunities for meaningful employment, decent housing, affordable child care, health care, family recreation, continued learning, and basic opportunities for their children. In the midst of unprecedented homelessness, urban joblessness, and child poverty, we are seeing a parallel indifference and hardening of the heart on the part of our society with regard to poor city children and their families. The result of these assumptions is less responsiveness to already critical conditions. For example, the myth of the welfare queen (Zucchino 1997) still abounds, assuming that mothers in poverty are leeches on the welfare system, smoking cigarettes and watching television all day, unconcerned about the education of their "many" children. Stereotypes such as this have led to the elimination of what was at least a partial safety net for children in poverty. Such uninformed "reforms" have increased the poverty and desperation of 21 percent of the children in the United States.

This welfare reform "solution," much like the high-stakes testing "solution," has created many more problems than it attempts to solve (Beckman and Simonn 1999; Children's Defense Fund 2000). In *Celebrating City Teachers*, we will explore nonproblematic solutions, and we'll look closely at some excellent models for successful city teaching and learning.

Outline of the Book

Chapter 1 takes a look at the perspectives and strategies of teachers from two schools in Philadelphia. Four city teachers share their stories, their personal and collaborative journeys, and their visions of successful teaching and learning for all students. Interviews and classroom observations provide a view inside the classroom.

Chapter 2 describes the ecology of city teachers and the common themes that emerged as significant for teaching and learning in urban schools.

In Chapter 3 we visit teachers in the Taylor Elementary School, including observation and interview data from teachers, parents, students, school leaders, and community members. First impressions, themes, and principles of the school are described. The chapter concludes with stories from the family in the community with whom the author lived.

In Chapter 4 we visit teachers from the Harrington Elementary School, connecting with the parallel relationship and orchestration-of-learning themes, and discussing a metaphor of the school. The content of literacy teaching is described as an important part of successful teaching and learning.

Even in a "successful" school there are failures, "warts," barriers, and difficulties; and Chapter 5 explores some of these. A low-progress learner provides a glimpse of both the barriers and the possibilities for successful teaching, learning, and evaluating. We also take a look at the problematic solutions of standardization and testing as they impact upon city children, teachers, and schools.

Chapter 6 turns to the issue of creating new professionals for successful city teaching and learning. We describe a community-school-college partnership that becomes a resource not only for reclaiming African American and Latino youth, but also for developing future teachers for diverse classrooms.

We conclude in Chapter 7 with a discussion of what can be done. Suggestions for teachers, parents, community members, college students, policymakers, and other citizens are offered to begin an ongoing dialogue on education for social justice and transformational change.

At the end of each chapter there is a place for reflection on ideas that might have stood out for you as a reader. These lists are meant as a starting place. I urge you to create your own.

This book follows my own personal journey of observing, questioning, listening, and learning in the city. Spending a year with teachers, parents, and children in urban elementary schools and communities gave me the opportunity to personally dispel many myths and stereotypes. This book is written in the hope of helping others to do the same. It asks the question, What can we learn from an ecological view of city teachers, schools, families, and communities? To answer this, it also asks:

> What is fact and what is fiction concerning city teachers and city schools?
>
> What is the basis for our negative assumptions and stereotypes about city teachers, schools, and their communities?
>
> What is fact and what is fiction concerning urban families and urban communities?
>
> How can we meaningfully evaluate learning in city schools?
>
> How do race, class, language, and culture interface with city teaching and learning?
>
> What makes it possible for strong family and school relationships to be built across race, class, language, and culture?
>
> What are the beliefs, values, philosophies, practices, and strategies of teachers and teacher leaders in city schools?

How do city teachers evaluate and teach reading and writing?

What are the relationships, the school climate, and the environment for learning like in city schools?

How do city teachers and city schools link with families and the community in support of children?

How can we prepare new city teachers to be successful with their students and families?

What can we do to support the dedicated, inspiring work of city teachers who are on the front lines?

These are some of the questions explored in the chapters to follow. As a group of collaborating teachers, mothers, and urban community members, my colleagues and I continue in our struggle to learn more about city teaching and learning, about successfully teaching reading and writing, and about preparing new teachers to create an ecology of success for urban children. The stories to follow are less stories of individual heroism than they are stories of collective struggle, resistance, and advocacy for city children and for their right to education, health, and well-being as described in the Universal Declaration of Human Rights (United Nations 1948).

1

City Teachers
Beliefs, Stories, and Mother Wit

IN COLLABORATION WITH TERESA ALVAREZ, DEBORAH WILLIAMS,
LINDA KIDD, AND DEBBIE WILLIAMS

The best metaphor that I have heard for trying to capture the artistry, energy, and passion of the teachers that I have had the honor to observe, interview, and work with over the past five years was used by Gloria Ladson-Billings in describing the pedagogy of the Black Preacher: it's like trying to capture lightning in a bottle. So the collection of interview data, classroom observations, and quotations from teacher presentations that follows must be seen as a mere sketch of what is in reality a rich mosaic, essentially impossible to describe.

In March of 1998 and 2000, at the University of Pennsylvania's Ethnography in Education Research Forum in Philadelphia, four teachers from the Taylor and Harrington Elementary Schools talked about what they know, believe, and do. Deborah Williams and Teresa Alvarez from Taylor presented, along with Linda Kidd and Debbie Williams from Harrington. Also speaking were Carol Hirschfeld, a former Harrington reading teacher (currently a language arts cluster facilitator in Philadelphia), and Wendy Shapiro, a former principal at Taylor (currently a cluster leader in Philadelphia). They spoke with groups of teachers, teacher educators, and qualitative researchers from across the country, as well as from Canada, South America, Australia, Europe, and the Caribbean, who had been studying schooling for many years.

They shared both what they believe and what they do to ensure the success of their students, their presentations laced generously with stories, "mother wit," and advice for preparing new teachers. The audience responses were overwhelmingly enthusiastic, with questions that ranged from the practical to the philosophical, most expressing awe at what these teachers have been doing for the past several decades of their lives. (We estimated that the combined total of the four teachers' years of service was over a century.)

In this chapter I have combined teacher observations and interviews from 1996 to 2000 with presentations to audiences at the Ethnography Forums and the spring 2000 NCTE (National Council of Teachers of English) Conference in New York City. My students from Elizabethtown College, who either visited city classrooms with me over the past five years, heard audiotaped interviews of the teachers, or saw their videotaped presentations, have been deeply inspired by these city teachers. And their enthusiastic responses suggest to me the value of teacher-to-teacher sharing of the "secrets of the dreamkeepers," to borrow again from Gloria Ladson-Billings (1994), and of making such exchanges an integral part of teacher-preparation programs.

Deborah Williams, Taylor Elementary School

Debby's classroom is a mixed first- and second-grade class. She and a few other teachers formed a small learning community that uses a nongraded approach to teaching. She believes that each child should have a chance to experience success, an opportunity that traditional grading and testing may deny. Rather than using a traditional grading system for her group of "off-schedule" students, she employs a descriptive report card along with a variety of other forms of evaluation that value learners' strengths and potentials, similar to those advocated in the work of Jane Hansen (1987, 1998) and Pat Carini (1979, 1996).

> We have looked at assessments in a different manner in our school. And we've been working diligently for the last four or five years with professional development, looking within ourselves and restructuring, to say, you know, we need to start assessing the children in a different way. The old way is not gonna fly. The circle is going to be broken. It's not going to go around and around anymore, because we're getting a new breed of children.
>
> We all agree on that. But [we are] not getting away from the standards. And [our approach to change] is not a phobia—it's not fearful. It is for you to go with the trekking—go beyond what you see, and investigate, and you can be successful in your teaching career in the inner-city schools.

Donning her black baseball cap with roses, Debby expressively shares a Red Riding Hood story with her students in a circle on the rug, encouraging them to think and talk about the story with her. She asks them to "Put on your thinking caps," and all hands go eagerly to their heads, slipping on their imaginary hats. After the story, Debby tells her students, "I'll have a surprise for you tomorrow—another Red Riding Hood story from Europe!"

She talks with them enthusiastically about comparing stories, and encourages them to use the technique outside of class: "When you use that word [*compare*] at home," she tells them, "they'll think you're a fifth grader!" Students move from whole-group story sharing to their small literature-study groups, formed around the books they have chosen. Yesterday they "shopped" for a book, chose one, sat with others who chose the same book, and read the books together.

Today Debby is modeling problem solving and question asking. She reminds them about what to do if you don't know a word: look at the accompanying picture, ask a friend, sound it out, or follow along as another person reads it. She talks with them about the five Ws (who, what, when, where, why), which she puts on a chart pad. And she invites them to ask her a question about the book they are reading, then reminds them, "This is what you will do in your group."

As Debby moves from group to group, she models with her students the reading and questioning process, continually coaching and encouraging them. I watch her face light up as she tells one group, "That's pretty good!" and as she joyfully raises both hands in delight with another group's questions.

One of Debby's classroom-management methods is speaking in a very soft voice, which requires her students to get very quiet in order to hear her. Or she may turn the lights off for a moment to get the class' attention. She also reminds her students, as she walks around the room, "While I'm wearing my hat, you can't call my name." Thus, they know they are to work collaboratively.

She shows me the "new secret" of the class: a silent clap, performed with two fingers. When it is time for lunch, and everyone is to be quiet and in their seats, Debby holds up a pin playfully and says, "Let's see if I can hear this pin drop."

Earlier in the morning, she had referred to a wall chart on listening.

Listening looks like . . .
    eye contact
    turn your head to listen
    mouths closed

Listening sounds like . . .
    one voice at a time

Thank you for telling me that
Um hum
Please say that again
That was a great story

Debby Williams has strong ideas about children and learning.

I think one of the most unique things about my classroom and my beliefs is that I believe all children can learn. I really, really believe that children come with prior knowledge. We all learn that in a textbook, but we don't apply it in many cases.

So we have to begin by looking within each child and realizing, This is a walking book of knowledge! And we are the key to finding how to unlock that book, and let that knowledge seep out into the atmosphere.

So in my belief, I really try to approach my teaching in the classroom with a different attitude, one that encourages everyone to take risks. In teaching reading, I really believe in the literature approach to teaching children how to read. I believe that in a book, there's a thousand . . . million . . . things waiting to be released.

And so the children begin to facilitate the learning as you expose them to one concept. The concept that children are to be listeners only, and not speakers—I totally threw that in the trash. I said, "No—I believe children have something within them."

So one of the things that I do that is a very important part of my class is, we begin with the morning circle. And from the circle, many things are discussed—the neighborhood, the school, things that they like, their hobbies, people that they adore, things they like to eat. Very, very interesting conversation goes on, and I take the opportunity to seize the moment, and throw the skills in there. While we're all talking about things that we love to do and books that we like to read, I begin to incorporate the literature skills that I want to teach them in the following week or month.

So my mornings are a time to connect with the children. I think one of the things that you should know, as a new teacher, is that you must connect with your children. And it can be done very easily, just through literature. And one way is to let them develop their listening and speaking skills. If you begin to let them talk, the knowledge that they have will begin to seep out, and you will be able to take that knowledge and facilitate the learning.

> As a teacher I really believe in long-range planning—looking ahead. We know our focus; we know what's expected, above and beyond Taylor Elementary. We know what the state says. We know the mandates. We know the standards. How do we get there? How do you make this applicable for your students? The way you do it is through *them,* by becoming a teacher who is a listener and a planner.

Another day in class Debby emphasizes the role of the team captain, the student responsible for returning books and collecting materials. She tells them to take responsibility for helping their team, rewarding one team for working well together, and reminding them that responsibility is "in your heart and in your brain." I notice that the team captains begin to take more responsibility, and that others begin to listen and contribute more effectively to the group.

Coaching one group, Debby asks, "What was the problem in the story?" When a student responds, Debby asks, "What sentence tells you that that is a problem?" Later she encourages a student to extend her short response to a question, by asking, "Can you tell me more?" and, "Why would you think that?" The result is a much fuller explanation from the student, to which Debby enthusiastically responds, "Very good—give her a hand!" as she models the silent two-finger clap.

When one student tries to answer for another student, Debby says, "I want Diana on the stage. She's in the spotlight now." Each student is given the chance to shine, and the expectations for success are high. Debby points out to me Marquita, who is reading expressively and with enthusiasm. She has progressed from primer to second-grade reading level this year.

There are two clotheslines strung across Debby's classroom, where student artwork and writing are proudly displayed, along with informative charts on editing symbols and rules for punctuation and capitalization. Students make their own lists of words they have trouble with, make flash cards with these, and take them home to study.

Debby explains that she uses the children's language in the classroom and links with their parents in a variety of ways. She also offers helpful advice for new city teachers.

> We have an excellent parent-support system in our school. We have established a monthly meeting with our parents in my community, which I do with another teacher. They come in once a month, and in that monthly meeting we may discuss trips, or we talk about the upcoming events in the school. And

then we will hold another meeting with all the parents within my own room.

And I do a workshop. I train my parents how to become my partners. As a teacher in Philadelphia, you need to become your parents' partner in educating their child. And the way that you do that is to have them come in, meet the staff, and you go out and learn the community. Get a hold on the environment.

Come in, take a day, and just go around the neighborhood. Find out the businesses, the physical outlay of the buildings, and then come back in your own four walls, and begin to create a plan. Make it a part of you. As much of yourself that you share with the children is as much as they'll give to you.

I'm really personal with my kids. We are a feely, lovey, huggy class. And I'm successful with them because they know that I care. And I tell them why I came. Many of the students don't know why you come and stand in front of them. So they begin to pour out what they know, and you take that as a stepping board, and you begin to develop the learning.

Debby attributes her growing expertise in literature-based reading and writing processes to courses that she has taken, such as the Penn Literacy Network from The University of Pennsylvania and reading courses at St. Joseph's University. Her small-group reading materials follow Marie Clay's (1993) Reading Recovery approach, with careful teacher observation and documentation using "little books" that progress in difficulty.

Does Debby like teaching? Here is what she says:

It is a heartbeat that, if you're for it, you need to jump into it. And I really can tell you that it's rewarding. I love what I do. I would never, ever think of doing anything else except teaching and touching minds. We do touch minds.

Deborah Williams, Harrington Elementary School

A source of confusion both to my college students and to the people who put together the programs for our teacher presentations was the fact that there are two Deborah Williams in the Philadelphia School District: Debby at the Taylor School in North Philadelphia and Debbie at the Harrington School in West Philadelphia. Both are African American women, and both are excellent teachers whom I have had the opportunity to have as research colleagues. I have purposefully arranged their stories one after the other in this chapter so that readers can appreciate their uniqueness and differences as well as their similarities.

As I walk into Debbie Williams' classroom at Harrington, I see a collection of string instruments in one corner (a cello, violin, base violin, guitar, banjo) and one wall filled with pictures of African American musicians. Outside Debbie's room, the hallway is filled with African musical instruments that the children and their parents have made—full-wall displays that celebrate community learning linked with classroom learning.

Debbie's position this year is in music for the whole school, and she loves it. She tells me that she began the year with rap music, and that the kids were impressed that she knew the names of the rap artists and their songs. She moved to other famous African American musicians, "slipping in," she says, some opera too.

They are reviewing the previous day's lesson, and in her lively and animated way she engages the students in talking with her and writing about it. They take a break for a few minutes to show me the movements they did during a recent assembly performance to "I Believe I Can Fly" (R. Kelly's song from the movie *Space Jam*). Debbie leads them in a combination of dance steps and movements, encouraging them to "really get into it," and her students mimic the energetic, whole-body movements of rock and pop singers—their eyes and faces alive with enthusiasm, their bodies dancing to the rhythm of the music, their arms outstretched. The song lyrics match their gestures of spreading their wings to fly away. They sing of believing they can soar and achieve miracles. And in their performance they affirm that, if they can see it, they can do it—if they believe it, there is nothing to it.

The joy and hope in their beautiful faces moves me to tears. They are sharing the dreams for their own lives so eloquently, so hopefully, and so expressively. And these dreams are brought meaningfully into their school curriculum by a talented, committed teacher who believes in her students' abilities, sees their strengths, and works to ensure that they reach their potentials.

At the Ethnography Forum, Debbie illustrated the ways that she uses the language of her African American students in the classroom. She and Linda Kidd from Harrington demonstrated the use of Ebonics through several short dialogues. She asked Linda first to speak with her in Standard English, then in Ebonics.

Debbie (D): Linda, how are you today?
Linda (L): Well, I feel wonderful.
D: And how are the children, Linda?
L: Oh, they're wonderful too.
D: Good, well I hope you'll have a great day.
L: And I hope the same for you.

Okay, now let's put it in Ebonics.

D: Lin!
L: Yeah?
D: Hey!
L: Hey, what's happenin' girl?
D: See you later!
L: All right!

We said the same thing! Because communication is through the person you're communicating with understanding what you're saying. I cut out all that other stuff. Now to me, also, if a person wants to know further information, then you will give it to them, and they will ask for it. If I said to Linda—Linda, speak to me in Ebonics—

D: Hey!
L: Hey, what's happenin'?
D: Not too good today.

Then she gets a signal to ask me further. Other than that, there's no need to say a lot of words. I was raised by my grandmother, and she spoke two or three words. We were made to feel, when we went to school, that [speaking] two or three words was inappropriate: "Go here." Commands like, "Do this." Everything [at home] was in short sentences.

But I knew what my grandmother meant. And the reason why I did [was] because Ebonics is not just speaking. It's language. The body language is incorporated into Ebonics. How is the body language incorporated?

I saw Jill the other day. Jill came in and she said, "How're you doing Mrs. Williams?" I said, "Hey!" Walked over to her. She *hugged* me. Even though she doesn't speak Ebonics, she knew through the body language. It's not just the words!

African Americans can look at a child [in a way that says] "Stop." Am I right African Americans? [laughter from the audience] And they know, because the body language, and the pointing, the eyes popping. Where, if you don't understand that language: "Sit down junior! Let me speak to your mother!" I hear them sometimes. "Do you want me to call your mother?"

And the African American junior says, "Oh *please!*"

They get the message sometimes with just a short amount of words. Again, I'm not saying that I teach Ebonics. I'm saying, you have to be aware. So when the child doesn't answer you in a complete sentence, [there is] nothing wrong with that child's language. We talk as little as we can. I've had to pad in my language.

I went to college as an older woman, after my children were grown up, and I had to pad in "however," and "therefore," and "basically," and, "Excuse me professor (at Temple) would you please hold that elevator?"

Debbie described one time when she was running late and she forgot the Standard English in her haste to catch an elevator: "I said, 'Yo! Hold that elevator!' They smiled, and they held it. I didn't have time to go into a lot of long stuff, or the elevator door would have closed!"

Then she shared a story about a class trip to Washington:

I had the privilege last year of taking my class to Washington, D.C. And I had already given the rules, before the children got on the bus. And they were getting a little noisy. We had parents on there, and I was sitting in the front.

I just stood up, and I said, "Why am I standing up?" And I sat back down.

When we got off at the stop, the bus driver, who was Caucasian, said, "What's the name of that game?"

And I said, "What game?"

He said, "You were playing a game on the bus, but I never got to understand what the game was."

He was really sincere. And I said to him, "Well, what did I say?"

He said, "You stood up and you said, 'Why am I standing up?' And everything got quiet. And I was waiting for the rest. . . ."

I said, "No. Every African American—all my children are African Americans—they *knew* why I was standing up. 'Shut up!' That's what it meant."

But they just knew that. I didn't have to go, "I'm not going to speak about all that talking back there," and whatever. "Why am I standing up?" with the body talk, with the gestures, and the eyes popping. The kids knew. Okay, they started talking about a half an hour later, but it was good for a half an hour.

Debbie's advice concerning Ebonics and teacher preparation is as follows:

I'm not an advocate of Ebonics being taught in the classroom. But here is what I say: I feel that the colleges, when they are preparing their teachers, should prepare them to recognize Ebonics when they hear it. Accept Ebonics as a valid form of communication in the African American community. Know that it is there—there's nothing wrong with that language.

Sometimes we say there's something wrong with the kids' language, because there are so many inconsistencies when it comes to *ing*'s, and there are so many rules in the language, where Ebonics is direct and to the point.

The people were brought here as slaves, and they had to learn the language as best they could. . . . They had to learn a language and they had to incorporate it the best they could from the white slave masters. So as a result of that . . . they interpret it from their language to this language. So the *d*'s were left off, the *s*'s, and the *ing*'s.

Do a little research on that, teachers. You really need to know the children, and do a little research in terms of what that background is. I think they should prepare teachers to build on Ebonics to move the kids to Standard English. Like Deborah [from Taylor] said, "Let the children speak."

You can let the children get into the story, because our culture's based on call and answer. That answer and call—yes, it's in a minister's situation. If you go into an African American church, and you stand up there [in a flat tone]: "Now we're talking about this thing today, and you know Jesus is the only one, and whatever, whatever." And you continue to talk [that way], we'll say, "This minister needs to get *into* it." Because Ebonics is also emotionalism! If I say [with spirit], "Hello, how are you today? Amen!" there is some kind of call. I call it and you answer—it's a response.

Now the last thing I want to say about Ebonics is, be able to understand your children's parents, who may speak in Ebonics.

Communicate effectively with them. If I'm talking to a parent who does not speak Standard English well, but believe me they speak Ebonics well, I don't mean that you have to speak in Ebonics. But be aware of what they're saying, and try to tone down your language. Because you might come off from another direction. It does not mean [you must] get rid of your professionalism. For example, [in] August—a phone call:

> *D:* Hey! I'm Ms. Williams.
> *Parent:* Who's Ms. Wiliams?
> *D:* I'll have your child in September. Look, meet me the first day, so I can let you know what I'm gonna be all about.

Just like that I say it. Cause that's my clientele. Those are the ones [who are] gonna help me get through the school system. Those are the ones [who] are going to back me up. Parents get that feeling that you have already jumped right on their bandwagon: "Come in the first day of school and meet me." I've done this for years: "Look me over. See how I look. What perfume I use."

But that first day of school, everybody's represented. And I tell the parents, "If you're working, send me Cousin George, the family dog, send me *somebody* that can represent your child." The first day of school, my parents walk in with my children. It's too late when you wait for the Back to School Night. You have to get that personal relationship with the parents. The principal cannot do that. All they can do is hope the parents come out, and by then the parents are mad, the teachers are mad, and everybody's angry—they don't come to the meeting.

But if you get them [early]—they're gonna come and look you over and say, "Who is this calling me in August?" Then they come, and let them know. And you speak . . . speak natural—cut down the words some. Let the parents respond to you. Tell them what you expect. And let them know at the end, "You do this for me, and I promise you you're gonna get a good product."

Amen!

Linda Kidd, Harrington Elementary School

In Linda Kidd's classroom, next door to Debbie Williams, she is showing the film of Alex Haley's *Roots*. As the class watches the movie, she tells me that her students did a great job presenting a variety of careers in poetry form at the recent assembly. They dressed as a teacher, nurse, doctor, writer, or other professionals, and recited a poem about that career for the school.

In the front of the room is a Venn diagram of Bessie Coleman and Amelia Earhart, famous Black and White women pilots whom they were discussing earlier. One corner of Linda's room is filled with books about famous African Americans—books her students read to do the collection of reports they have just turned in to her.

Linda wants her students to be surrounded with the struggles and accomplishments of other African Americans so that they are inspired to continue the struggle—to be all that they can be, even in the face of great difficulties. She wants them to see themselves as teachers, doctors, lawyers, and writers—as proud and brilliant as the famous people they have been studying.

The students' reports are on Rosa Parks, Frederick Douglass, Mae Jenison, Zora Neale Hurston, Shirley Chisolm, Bessie Coleman, Harriet Tubman, Barbara Jordan, and other famous African Americans. She allows them to do dioramas as an alternative to writing the report. When Linda's students study Africa, they learn about the griots and their wonderful stories, the kings in Africa, and the regal heritage of all African Americans. Together with Debbie Williams, Linda developed a six-month thematic unit on Africa for the entire Harrington School. She described both the collaboration and the unit at the Ethnography Forum in 1998.

My name is Linda Kidd, and I'm the social studies teacher for Harrington Elementary School, where I've been for twenty-eight years. But I have a unique situation: now I'm teaching social studies to all the children from kindergarten to fourth. And it is indeed a task—it's a real big challenge, but I enjoy it, I really do.

And Debbie has helped me out a lot. So what I have to say to you is that [through] collaborative effort between us, we've both really grown a lot in the last three or four years.

But when you think in terms of teaching African American children, certainly I'm going to jump on the component about parents. You must make them your allies. It's absolutely imperative. What we have found to be very successful, after you meet them, and after you interact with them, is to set up a workshop. And we set up this workshop with the purpose of enlightening parents as to what we're going to do.

We had an idea that we wanted to develop a thematic unit on Africa. We wanted our children to really know where our roots started and began. So with that, I am a talker—I am very artistic. But I am not musically inclined or rhythmically inclined, at all. So I went to my neighbor, who is definitely very strong in those areas. So I would advise teachers, when you know you have a weak area, go to the experts. When we were in school, we always found a smart kid who knew what they were doing to be our buddy—or at least to tutor us.

The same thing happens in the professional realm. You go to the teacher who has those strengths, and then you collaborate. I went to Debbie and said, "I want a musical component to this. You can't teach Africa without music. You simply cannot do it."

She loved the idea: "Oh yeah, well give me a weekend to think about it." So she did. And what we decided to do was, first we would feed every class in the school into her room. And then I would take her class. So we had to reorganize and reschedule and replan. But it worked out beautifully. We also had a lesson plan to hand the teacher, so that she would know what direction we were going in, what we're about, what it's supposed to be, and what they can do to embellish it in their classrooms. We also had hands-on instruments for all the students. Every child that came in there had something that they could put their hands on. And Debbie taught a fabulous lesson.

Well, certainly they all went home and the word got out. So that is another thing I would like to advise everyone. Advertise—just like out in the public. You must advertise what you are doing in your classroom. You have to let people know what you are doing. Because what happens is, the cleaning lady sent us stuff, a volunteer sent us stuff, the principal brought in this big authentic African drum, and parents came and brought instruments so we had enough for the children.

Everyone jumped on board. I told my secretary what I wanted to do. She said, "No problem." I wanted her to make one outfit. She said, "Now, you know all the boys and girls don't come in one size." So she made an outfit like a dashiki for kindergarten up to fourth grade. And I asked her for a dashiki for a little boy, and she said, "Well you know the girls want to look good too." She had all this material that she had at home. And she made little outfits for the girls—just like the kimono—you put your arms in and wrapped it up. So they looked authentic.

What was so inspiring was that, when I went back into the kindergarten, and I asked, "You know, we're gonna be griots today, and who's gonna be the first volunteer to stand up and tell us a story?" Well, naturally I thought they'd be telling us about the Three Little Bears, or the Three Little Pigs, or Cinderella. They stood up, in every class—cause I have four kindergartens—and told the story that I had told them the previous week about Sundiata. And it was the most marvelous, inspiring time of my career.

But that's what happens, so you found out that they comprehended, and they could associate, and they could relate. Taking it even further, yes, we did map skills with the children from kindergarten to fourth. Certainly it gets a little more detailed with the upper grades, but you still can do it with kindergartners.

Thematic teaching and hands-on activities are very, very important for addressing all the different abilities and reading levels. And everyone can stay on task and contribute to the end product. So I do vary my approaches. Sometimes I do have to lecture, but I try to make history come alive. I try to take on that persona or that personality that I'm talking about. I try to put the children in that frame of mind, because I know they're like six and seven years old, and all they can be concerned about is, When's recess?

So it's very difficult to get them into a time period of hundreds and thousands of years gone by, because it's very difficult for adults. But I do try to do that by bringing it alive to them, but also with hands-on activities. And then when it comes to assessment, readily they can remember what they made, what they did, how they approached it.

And when you're talking in terms of writing, certainly I'm the scribe for the kindergartners. But if you keep that student's vocabulary, they'll read it back to you. And I found that to be really inspiring, because they have wonderful ideas; and I put their initials beside their concept or their idea, and certainly they'll remember it.

Teaching can be wonderful, and it's very inspiring. But you have to keep it alive. If you keep varying your curriculum, if you really do a lot of research, if you come from a different angle—you keep it alive for *you*, and then you can bring that enthusiasm to your classroom.

Teresa Alvarez, Taylor Elementary School

The following transcription is from Teresa's 1998 presentation at the Ethnography Forum, in which she talked about celebrating the culture and language of the community as a way to create successful learning for her Puerto Rican children and families.

I feel that my classroom is sort of like a celebration of all these things: language, the environment, the units that we put together, the parents, the activities, and of course our music. This is not just particular to my classroom, but this happens throughout Taylor School. It's a celebration of the students' language. My classroom is a bilingual classroom. I teach first and second grade—a split classroom—and I teach in Spanish. And ESL is a very important component of the classroom.

The environment: when you walk into my classroom, it's sort of like what Jill just said: "Welcome to our living room." I try to make the classroom a place where the children are comfortable, where they're motivated, where they want to be there. Because I feel that if they want to be there, they will be there and they will learn. And I feel that every single child that goes through that door into my classroom can learn and will learn. I think it's the expectations that I set for them that make them want to be there.

I develop my units with their culture in mind. I have presently twenty-three students. Twenty-one of them are from Puerto Rico, I have a student from Nicaragua, and a student from the Dominican Republic. There's a little corner in our room that says: "We celebrate our culture." It's just two bulletin boards, they're both under a window, and they have little things from Puerto Rico, a few things from Nicaragua, and a few things from the Dominican Republic. And these are things that either I had been able to get myself, or the children have brought in themselves. And we just decorate the room.

I'll share just one experience of a student who came into my classroom. The young man was very upset. He didn't want to be there—he wanted to go back to Puerto Rico. And he stood at the door, crying hysterically with Mom. He did not want to be there—he came from another school in November.

And I said, "You know what? You're going to love it here—just come into our room." And I walked him into the room, walked him toward the back of the room, and he looked and he said, "Mira—Puerto Rico!"

He saw the maps back there, and he just picked up a book that said, "Como estamos Puerto Rico," and he started asking me questions: "Missy, where are you from?" and, "This is where I am from!" And he loves it—he loves the classroom. In fact, they're moving and he doesn't want to go to another school.

So that's the environment. The units are thematic units that I have put together. Presently we're working on a "home" unit, so I try to incorporate how the houses are in Puerto Rico, or in Nicaragua, or in the Dominican Republic. I try to have children share, bring pictures in. We write letters to their families in Puerto Rico and try to get responses. And this is done in Spanish.

I feel the parents are a very, very important part of what happens in my classroom, and in our school. But in particular in my classroom the parents are invited to come in. They're asked to come in and share their knowledge, because they have so much.

I was born in Puerto Rico, but I came here when I was three years old. So the parents who have recently arrived from Puerto Rico with the students have so much that they can share with me—so many things. They bring in books, they bring in pictures for me, and they bring in videos that I can share with the classroom.

The activities that we do: We celebrate Three Kings Day. And this is done schoolwide, but it's also done in my classroom. We bring in the food, we bring in all the favorite little things that the children connect to their island and to what they left behind.

And the music is just something that I feel is very important in their lives, because they listen to it when they go home. They listen to it every day. And what I have is little cassettes or CDs that I bring in. They bring in their own music, too. Usually every day after recess we come upstairs and we just sit down and we listen to the music.

It just makes an environment that is really relaxing and enjoyable. I played one the other day, and the student said, "Missy, when I was in preschool I learned this in Puerto Rico!" So they know the songs—they sing along.

At the same time we're learning English. I do a lot of English instruction with them. I don't want you to think this is totally in Spanish, and they're not learning English—they are. And they're wonderful at it. I think they're very successful. And it's just a great place to be for the students.

REFLECTION: WHAT STOOD OUT FOR ME?

☐ Teachers can celebrate the language and culture of students and their families, and use this as a resource for teaching and learning.

☐ Teachers can connect with parents in respectful and meaningful ways, sharing their ideas for successful teaching and learning.

☐ Teachers who understand that music, art, and language are a vital part of who we are as human beings can create many opportunities for students' own musical, artistic, and linguistic expressions.

☐ Teachers can create a personally meaningful, comfortable, and inviting classroom environment.

☐ Teachers can find multiple ways for their students to demonstrate what they have learned, and can support that learning with love and care.

☐ Teachers who believe that their students can fly can help them see the breadth of opportunities available to them—teachers can be the wind beneath the spreading wings of their students.

2

The Ecology of City Teachers

Trying to understand city teachers and city schools apart from their ecology is like trying to fully understand pandas by studying them in a zoo. No serious biologist would study a living, interactive, interconnected organism or species apart from the environment in which it exists, at least not if they wanted valid and reliable information. Certainly they would not if they wanted to develop a contextually grounded and meaningful understanding of the species. And certainly they would not if that species were endangered. So the chapters to follow will attempt to place city teachers in their ecological contexts—their schools and communities—in the hope of attaining a richer understanding of the remarkable teaching and learning that they orchestrate on a daily basis.

Problems caused by studying teaching and learning outside their contexts are legion. They range from the illiterate attempts of policymakers to rank and judge the work of teachers (without ever observing them in the classroom or examining the quality of the ongoing daily work of their students) to the erroneous assumption that the learning of students can be meaningfully and usefully assessed in isolation from the ecological context in which it occurs. A continuation of such practices threatens the ecology of successful city teachers and their students. Our problematic "solutions" have, in fact, created an endangered species.

For the past fifteen years I have used the term *ecology* to describe the complex interrelationships of school, family, community, and culture that shape the learning of human beings (see Bartoli and Botel 1988 and Bartoli 1995 for discussions of this ecological approach and its sources in research and theory). In developing this concept, and in attempting to take an ecological approach to learning, I have been guided by Seymour Sarason's (1971, 1990, 1996, 1999) notion of the school as a complex cultural system, Urie Bronfenbrenner's (1979) description of interconnected subsystems in the ecology of human development, Nicholas Hobbs' (1978) description of an ecosystem for children, Gregory Bateson's (1972) *Steps to an Ecology of Mind* and theories on human communication, and by a family systems / family therapy approach to understanding human behavior (Hoffman 1981; Napier and Whitaker 1978; Minuchin 1974; Haley 1981), which I studied during my doctoral years.

In describing the educational system, Sarason (1999) includes "teachers and administrators; boards of education; colleges and universities; state departments of education; national, state, and local legislators and executives; and, of course, parents" (163). To add to this complexity, there are historic, linguistic, cultural, economic, and social issues to be factored in, as well as the undeniable influence of family health and welfare on the learning of human beings.

The phrase *ecology of learning* suggests the broader context of interrelationships that shape and constrain human learning—the complex interdependencies that are vital for survival and crucial for human growth and meaning making in life as well as in language. The use of this phrase is my humble attempt to capture and describe the vast complexity of human learning and nonlearning that will forever elude even our best research and evaluation approaches.

Over thirty years ago in *The Culture of the School and the Problem of Change*, Seymour Sarason noted that we know far too little about the actual functioning of schools and school systems, which he described as very complex cultures. And schools are embedded in equally complex community and family cultures. To give some structure to this complexity, we will look first at the wider ecology of city schools, and then focus on several parallel themes that emerged as significant across the four city schools that I studied in Philadelphia and New York City. In this way I hope to illustrate some of the ways that the ecologies of city teachers and their students are endangered.

The Ecology of City Schools and Communities

At a time when it is estimated that at least two million people are homeless and over thirty million people, the majority of whom are children, are living in poverty (Children's Defense Fund 2000), and when "savage inequalities" (Kozol 1992) and unequal opportunity (Bartoli 1995) continue to be the experience of far too many low-income city children and families in the United States, it is time to seriously take stock and make changes. Couple these essentially third world conditions for city children with the narrowly conceived and destructive practice (endorsed by politicians and the general public) of imposing irrelevant, oppressive, socioeconomically and culturally biased standardized tests on economically disadvantaged children and schools, and we have a sure prescription for continued failure, despair, and hopelessness (Kohn 2000; McNeil 2000; Coles 1998; Taylor 1996).

Thankfully, amid all of this illiterate policy and against seemingly insurmountable odds, there continue to be committed teachers, principals, parents, and students who are managing not only to survive but to create successful environments for learning. They are doing this in spite of the system, however, not because of it.

In many inspiring ways these dedicated, compassionate, tremendously hardworking people are finding ways to help ensure that the children in their care will learn to love books and reading, will become authors who can express their own ideas and questions, and will become inquiring scientists and mathematicians. The students in these endangered environments are becoming future citizens who care about their communities as well as the communities of those who are different from them, and they are learning how to begin to change their worlds for the better.

Families, teachers, and community members are working with students in this grand effort, modeling their own commitment to advocacy and change. In and out of the classroom, teachers and principals are mentoring students to hear and understand the views of people who are different culturally, racially, and economically from them. In collaboration with families, teachers are guiding students to respect and care about others as well as themselves—to follow the golden rule of doing unto others as you would have them do unto you (a schoolwide theme in one of the schools).

Learning from Teachers Within Their Ecologies

After a semester of observing and interviewing at four city schools, I was rereading my classroom observation notebooks, interview transcripts, and fieldwork journals, with the intention of understanding what it is that makes these schools and teachers so successful. It was then that I began to notice that many of the themes associated with successful learning environments for students were the same as those for teacher learning environments.

As I began to make multiple lists of categories and themes, I found them to be identical to those that I, as a teacher, need to continue growing and learning—conditions that I had found myself yearning for at my own school. And as I thought about this more, I realized that these same conditions were what made it possible for teachers to create the successful learning environments for their students that I had been observing.

The following list of ten parallel themes is a condensation of what began as a coding nightmare—twenty-five major categories and thirty-eight subcategories. I called these "Parallels in the creation of successful environments for both teacher and student opportunities to learn."

1. Time for reflective dialogue: scheduled and planned as part of the program/curriculum
2. Support for risk-taking, experimentation, making mistakes as a natural part of learning
3. Choices and the freedom to make them
4. Ownership, personal responsibility, empowerment
5. Respect for abilities, beliefs, interests, and ways of knowing, learning, and being
6. Collaboration with peers and peer mentoring
7. Shared motivation and commitment to learning, growth, change, and improvement of self and others
8. Having the resources needed for learning
9. Trust
10. Hopefulness

So I stopped looking for particular kinds of practices and methods, or for particular philosophies of teaching reading and writing, and I began to look more closely at these broader conditions for creating successful learning environments for both students and teachers. Many of them had to do with the kinds of relationships that were created for both teachers and students—and, actually, for parents and principals as well. So the second half of the year I tried to look more closely at relationships, along with the organizational and environmental dynamics of the teachers and schools, and what I observed validated what I had noticed at midyear.

Themes and Categories

By the end of the year the list of parallel themes for students and teacher learning evolved into the following list. I checked these out with the teachers, parents, and principals in all four schools and found consensus. I called the themes "Parallels in student and teacher ecologies for successful learning."

1. Students and teachers are valued, appreciated, and celebrated.
2. Evaluation methods (portfolios, observation, work sampling) put value in the learning and growth of students and teachers.
3. Individual interests, needs, choices, and personal freedom are valued.
4. People are supported and cared for (with kindness, knowledge, resources, action).
5. There is time scheduled for reflective dialogue and critical thinking.
6. Risk-taking, experimentation, and making mistakes are supported.
7. Ownership, empowerment, and personal responsibility are evident.
8. Collaboration with peers and peer mentoring are common practices.
9. Respectful relationships and trust building exist across race, culture, and language.
10. A family environment and caring community atmosphere is pervasive.
11. There is a meaningful, authentic learning and growth process: learning is social, personal, interactive and integrated, transformative, experiential, and constructivist.
12. There is fun and humor: the school laughs.
13. The administration is responsive, problem-solving, and activist/proactive.
14. People work hard: they are persistent and hopeful activists and advocates.
15. Motivation and commitment to learning, growth, and change are strong.

16. There are enough human and material resources for learning and growth.
17. The learning environment is democratic and choice-filled with individual freedom.

I grouped these seventeen themes into three major categories, which made the tasks of coding, analyzing, and describing the data much more manageable. The three general categories are relationships, orchestration of learning, and environment for learning. Following is a brief sketch of how the seventeen themes were grouped into these categories.

1. Relationships that support learning
   Valuing, appreciating and celebrating each other
   Caring and support (with kindness, resources, knowledge, action)
   Empowerment
   Collaboration
   Respect and trust across race and culture
   Democracy and individual freedom

2. Orchestration of learning
   Time scheduled for reflection, critical thinking, collaboration
   Evaluation methods that value growth and strength
   Curriculum is meaningful and growthful: SPITE (Social, Personal, Integrative, Transforming, Ecological)
   Human and material resources are adequate
   Administration solves problems, responds, advocates

3. Environment for learning
   Risk taking, experimentation, and making mistakes are supported
   Commitment and motivation for change and growth are pervasive
   There is fun and humor—we like being here and enjoy our work
   People work hard and are hopeful activists
   Respectful, trusting, and caring community/family

I'll share just a few examples of some of the relationship themes that I noticed from interviews and observations.

Mardes, a mother in Harlem, shared with me the barriers of anger and distrust that her son's teacher and assistant had to break through to build a relationship with her. Her life had not been an easy one:

> When I came into this school, I was going through a lot. I had recently went to jail. . . . I was like a tigress over my cubs. You know, I wouldn't let nobody get close to them, let alone get close to me.

When I asked Mardes how the teachers broke through those barriers at Central Park East II, she told me about the ways that they made her son feel loved and cared for, that they cared for children as if they were their own, about their resistance to labeling her son, and of the "miracle" change in his learning. And she also talked about their persistence in building a relationship with her and making her feel comfortable. When I asked her what new teachers need to learn, she said:

> Most of all they need to learn to show the children that they can trust and depend on them. And just show them that they'll be there for them. . . . Establish that trust between the child, and also you gotta establish a certain level of trust with the parent as well.
>
> Don't leave the child lingerin' in limbo, so to speak, because then the child is suffering, and the parents also suffer with the child.

Her child's teacher told me that she is supported in her relationship work by a classroom assistant who can take over much of the teaching at the beginning of the year while she makes continual calls to parents. The school director, Bruce Kanze, had a phone placed in her room especially for this purpose, and for linking with social services.

I observed another example of teacher support at CPE II Elementary School in a staff meeting focused on a teacher who was struggling with managing a class of very difficult students. The entire staff spent two hours after school listening carefully to her problems, asking thoughtful questions, and offering possible solutions in a respectful and caring way. A teacher who at first appeared very discouraged and depressed emerged as a more confident, supported, and hopeful professional.

Being supported and cared for, being respected, feeling valued and appreciated as an individual, and having your needs met were pervasive themes in the four schools where I observed. All of this seemed to create an environment for respectful and trusting relationships, which in turn made it possible for successful teaching and learning to occur. In general, what was common across all four sites was a family environment—a caring community of learners who felt respected and supported.

My classroom observations, along with student comments about their schools and teachers, held many examples of students being valued and appreciated. As I observed during book sharing and circle time, student responses were valued as unique and interesting contributions to the community discussion, not as right or wrong answers.

Students who, I was later told, had behavior problems or had been considered for special education had thoughtful comments and insights into the literature being discussed. Their work was celebrated throughout the rooms and hallways as well as in folders and portfolios that were shared with parents. Both informal and formal staff reviews of children underscored the respect teachers had for their students and colleagues, and their willingness to spend time to support their learning.

Administrative support for teachers was evident in the interviews I conducted with principals as well as my observations of administrators during faculty meetings and staff development sessions. In describing the teachers, Gerald Cohen, the principal of PS 114 in Brooklyn, said:

> I just believe that the people in that classroom are the hardest-working professionals anywhere in the world, and the most important people in the entire universe are teachers. I believe that. I respect them more than any other group. And I try to treat them with that kind of respect.
>
> If there is anything they want . . . if there are other methods or ways that they're more comfortable with, we support it. They can try something; they can experiment in any way they want. They have our support. If it doesn't work, it doesn't work. That doesn't mean you failed. It means you tried something that wasn't successful. We'll try something else.

When teachers are respected in this way, and when administrators take the time to build supportive relationships with them as individuals, this same respectful relationship-building can be shared with the children and their families.

And PS 114 has built an exemplary partnership with families. One example of their partnership was the parent-run "sewing factory" at the school, which Gerry told me about when I first came to visit. There was massive overcrowding at PS 114, which was built for six hundred students but had a student population of twice that number. There were as many as forty-three students in first- and second-grade classrooms, and even the school library and gym had to be turned into classrooms.

So the parents got together and raised twelve thousand dollars to put minilibraries in every classroom, including many good paperback books. To protect these, a group of mothers brought their sewing machines into the school and sewed cloth bags for each of the twelve hundred students. This way the children had a special bag to take a book home to read each night as part of their excellent reading and writing program, which was developed in collaboration with the Teachers College Reading and Writing Project, directed by Lucy Calkins.

Relationship Themes

When I began to study teachers and schools in Philadelphia and New York City, I believed that respectful and trusting relationships were important enough to be one of the major criteria for choosing a school to study. What was a surprise to me, however, was the degree to which relationships emerged as important in the teaching and learning processes, challenging some of the other deeply held beliefs and values that I carried with me into the study.

Concerning the importance of this category, I would like to make the somewhat radical (for me) statement that I believe that success in learning depends less on specific teaching methods than it does on the quality of the relationships that are developed among teachers, students, parents, school leaders, communities, and societies. Furthermore, I believe that successful learning depends more on the enthusiasm, commitment, and caring that people bring to their work with students and families than it does upon specific methods or approaches.

This is radical for me because, after I went through the very painful process of unlearning my former skills-oriented English-teacher and reading-specialist training, I became rather passionate about more student-centered, integrated, wholistic approaches. This is not to say that I would advocate fragmented, decontextualized teaching and testing, as Chapter 5 will certainly demonstrate. But I've learned that the importance of caring and supportive people transcends the importance of methods.

What appeared repeatedly in my observation notebooks, fieldwork journals, memos, site documents, and interview transcripts were instances of supportive, mutually respectful, trusting human relationships. People cared about and supported each other with kindness, resources, knowledge, and personal action. They collaborated with each other, engaging in democratic decision making and respecting individual freedom of choice. Individual voices were heard and supported so that people felt empowered and appreciated, regardless of race, class, culture, or language.

As a result of this relationship building, a respectful, trusting, caring family environment was created within the classroom and school. There was support for risk taking, experimentation, and making mistakes. So commitment to and motivation for change and growth were pervasive. People worked hard and were hopeful activists in support of the children. And there was a spirit of fun and humor, with people feeling that they liked being there and they enjoyed their work.

The mutual respect and trust of people within these school ecologies cut across race, culture, and language divisions. People genuinely celebrated and valued each other rather than merely tolerating differences. Collaboration and democratic decision making were evident in the ways that people worked together toward the common goal of helping students become successful learners. And an approach valuing individual voices, choice, freedom, and empowerment did not neglect or sacrifice the common good for all children.

Chapters 3 and 4 provide many specific examples of this kind of supportive and empowering relationship building that provides the foundation for successful teaching and learning.

Orchestration of Learning Themes

In describing how teaching and learning are organized or structured, I use the term *orchestration* because it seems to better capture the dynamic artistry of teachers in the schools, not unlike Seymour Sarason's (1999) description of teaching as a performing art. I was struck by a difficult-to-describe musical and artistic quality of teaching in the schools, not only in the actual use of inspiring songs and the beautiful artwork of the students, but in the metaphoric sense of a symphony that is sometimes carefully orchestrated, and at other times more spontaneous, like improvisational jazz.

Beneath the methods and materials used in the classroom, and undergirding the classroom teaching and learning processes, are the larger issues of the content of the curriculum (Coles 1998; Freire 1981; Ladson-Billings 1994), the purpose and goals of the school (Dewey 1916, 1938), and the way learning is organized and orchestrated within the school—for both student and teacher learning and development. To the statement that relationships are more significant than methods, I will add that meaningful and challenging content and goals—the quality and depth of the curriculum—are more important than particular methodologies. As we will see in Chapters 3 and 4, the examples from teachers in their classrooms illustrate the importance of this orchestration of learning.

Learning from Successful City Teachers and Schools

We have so much to learn from these teachers, schools, and communities. This is not to say, however, that because they are doing good work and are successful in spite of the odds and in spite of an inequitable system, if all poor urban communities and schools adopted the same approach, our problems would be solved. The real solution must involve a more accurately informed and politically invested society, dedicated to the equality and democracy on which it was founded. Then we could talk about succeeding *because* of the system, rather than in spite of it.

What are some of the lessons to be learned from these city teachers and their elementary schools? What have they achieved and how have they achieved it? What are the ways in which ordinary people can do extraordinary things, in spite of multiple and persistent problems, including wrongheaded assessment policies, a lack of sufficient financial support, and a surplus of biases and prejudices that constantly negate and undermine their best efforts?

There are some answers to be found in the chapters to follow, as we look closely at teachers within the ecology of their urban elementary schools. These are endangered ecologies that are continually threatened, both internally and externally, by the lack of resources and social supports for poor families and by educationally unsound and politically imposed constraints. It is vital that we begin to support not only these teachers, schools, and communities, but also the thousands of others (both successful and unsuccessful) that they represent.

We cannot continue the destructive pattern of savage inequalities and unequal opportunity that have characterized schooling in the

United States for the past century. For if we do, our legacy for the twenty-first century will be the destruction of the very foundation of equality, democracy, and justice that was the dream of our forefathers, and the hope of past and present immigrants whose coming to America represented their striving for their highest ideals and goals. And, most tragically of all, we will have missed the very real opportunity for transformational change that these teachers, schools, and communities represent.

What will it take to make that change? At the least it will take a carefully constructed and collaboratively pursued plan of action that includes:

1. the support of currently successful efforts

2. the development and support—particularly from higher education, business, and government—of hundreds of other successful urban public schools and communities

3. the development of new professionals with a broader vision of both the problems of and the solutions for students placed at risk in underfunded urban schools and communities

4. a societal and political commitment to end the abusive and unconscionable child and family poverty that belies our democratic ideals

In Chapter 7 we will return to these and other vital change issues. But we turn next to an exploration of two city schools in Philadelphia and the teachers, students, parents, teacher leaders, and community members within them. The relationships, the orchestration of learning, and the overall climate or environment will serve as organizing categories of themes as we explore the ecology of the Taylor Elementary School in North Philadelphia and the Harrington Elementary School in West Philadelphia.

REFLECTION: WHAT STOOD OUT FOR ME?

☐ Teachers and students cannot be fully understood or meaning-fully evaluated apart from the ecology of their classrooms, schools, and communities.

☐ Supportive, respectful, and trusting relationships are a vital part of learning, and they are equally important for teachers, parents, and students.

☐ The quality, depth, and cultural relevance of the school curriculum are vital to successful learning.

☐ Equal educational opportunity for all demands an end to child and family poverty in the United States.

3

Teaching and Learning at Taylor
"Yes We Can!"

When I first visited Taylor Elementary School I felt a warm, welcoming breeze—the kind of soft, gentle, caressing, and enveloping warmth I've felt on Caribbean islands. And later I thought of the school as an island or oasis on a graffiti-laden, cold street, standing in stark contrast to the other buildings along Erie Avenue. The Puerto Rican culture as I have experienced it, both on the island or in the company of Puerto Rican people in the United States, feels like this to me in general: there are close, openly loving and embracing family relationships, and this warmth extends to family friends and to the larger community.

Before school, mothers, grandmothers, aunts, fathers, and children on the Taylor school yard smile and chat with one another, with the teachers, with the principal, and with me. They also hug one another, especially if a child is crying, or hurt, or just happy to see them. The air is filled with a melodic mixture of Spanish and English, and "welcome" and "buenos dias" are often spoken together.

I do not feel out of place or unwelcome, even though I do not speak Spanish; and those whose first language is Spanish appear to feel the same. Their Spanish language is used and celebrated, just as their children are celebrated, valued, and appreciated. The welcoming spirit of the school struck me on my very first visit to Taylor.

As I stood on the playground before school, that first day, surrounded by Puerto Rican children and community members who were greeted warmly in both languages (a practice that was continued in the classroom as parents came in and out at various times throughout the day), Taylor seemed like such a special place to be—respectful, warm, and caring.

In the spring of 1996 I heard Teresa Alvarez speak at the Ethnography in Education Forum about the Puerto Rican–culture focus of her second-grade bilingual classroom. This inspired me to visit her classroom, possibly as a contrast to another city school in which I observed little being done to celebrate the Puerto Rican history, culture, and language of the community (Bartoli 1995).

Teresa's teaching style is particularly respectful and caring toward both her students and their families. Having lived in the community and raised her own children there, she is known and trusted by the parents, who feel free to come to her (at her encouragement) with their questions, their problems, and their celebrations. Parents have also said that they feel free to approach the principal, Wendy Shapiro, who speaks their language and strives to both understand and help solve their problems.

Fortunately for me, an Anglo whose language learning was limited to French and Latin in school, Teresa's class assignment for the year that I observed was an English-instruction classroom rather than a bilingual classroom. I was also fortunate to have found in Teresa such a kind and patient research colleague; both in and out of the classroom, she graciously translated for me when she spoke Spanish with children and parents.

PART I: THE ECOLOGY OF TAYLOR

An Overview of Taylor

Bayard Taylor Elementary School is located in North Philadelphia at Erie Avenue and Randolph Street in a predominantly Puerto Rican community. The school, built in 1907, is a large old brick building surrounded by a macadam school yard. There is a high metal fence in the area where families wait for the teachers in the morning. There are 650 students in the school: 77 percent are Latino and 20 percent are African American.

An annex to the school is down the block on Erie Avenue, beside a Baptist church. There are some Chinese and Puerto Rican restaurants nearby, and there is a Spanish food truck parked across the street, where I buy my morning coffee. The traffic is problematic in the neighborhood around the school. High-volume boom boxes in cars can be heard (and felt) when they pass, and there is danger to the children and their families from the fast-moving vehicles.

Two weeks before I arrived in the fall, a little girl and her grandfather were hit by a car and killed as they walked to a nearby school. Parents were appealing to city hall for blinking lights and other traffic safety measures, and they were eventually successful in getting the traffic to slow down.

The classroom teaching methods involve much echo and choral reading that provides low-risk fluent reading practice for all children. There is also modeling by the teacher so that students are clear about what they are expected to do. Thematic units encourage faculty collaboration as well as student engagement and cooperation in the classroom, and students are encouraged to do their best and to become responsible, independent learners. Descriptive report cards allow a more observation-based form of evaluation than traditional grading systems.

Parents report feeling support from the teachers and the principal in their efforts to improve the school. One parent effort was an improved hot breakfast and lunch program led by the Eastern Philadelphia Organizing Project (EPOP) parent group. This group, supported by Gordon Witman as mediator/adviser and Ortencia Santiago as parent leader, was also working to confront a slumlord whose property beside the school yard is filled with trash and hazardous items that the children can easily come in contact with. EPOP was devising a plan to have the lot cleaned up and possibly donated to the school to be used as a reading garden.

Efficiency of the System

What struck me about Taylor was the openness and responsiveness of the school as a system. Schools that do not work very well tend to be closed systems, controlled by autocratic administrators and mandates, and unresponsive to the ideas of others within the system. By contrast, several times I observed an immediate response to situations at Taylor that in a closed system school would have been problematic for both teachers and students.

One example involved a non-English-speaking student who was at the begining of the year, placed in Teresa's English-instruction classroom, rather than in a bilingual classroom. The principal came to Teresa's classroom in one of her routine visits to welcome and greet students, and she saw the problem. Shortly thereafter, the student was placed in a bilingual classroom.

A second instance involved a proposed International Day to replace the traditional Halloween celebration. The principal and some of the faculty members who had come up with the idea suggested a whole-school thematic approach to the day, with each class researching a country and presenting its culture. Since many teachers were already planning for other thematic units, they saw this as an added burden—an inconvenience to or interruption of their teaching. After the faculty meeting announcement of the proposal, several faculty members wrote and talked to the principal, expressing their concerns.

The response was quick and appropriate. I was sitting in a small learning community (SLC) meeting on work sampling the following morning, listening to teachers discuss the problems posed by International Day. At the end of the meeting one of the members, who had left early, returned with a memo retrieved from her mailbox announcing that the day was canceled. The issue had been resolved and teachers felt listened to.

The continuous faculty development over the past several years at Taylor has been linked with the Penn Literacy Network and the writing project at the University of Pennsylvania, work sampling, the Coalition of Essential Schools principles, and to other student-centered approaches that use portfolios, inquiry learning, thematic units, and literature-based reading.

The tone at the faculty meetings is one of collaboration, shared enthusiasm, and a commitment to better learning for the children and to continuous improvement. You get a sense that the teachers and principal really care about the students and that they are taking full responsibility for their successful learning and growth. For example, when I observed a meeting of the faculty downtown at the school district office, they were a voice of advocacy for their children, particularly with respect to frustrating and harmful tests that they believe punish their Spanish-speaking students.

Relationships in the Classroom and School

I was impressed by the gentle and supportive treatment of children in the classroom. Crying or unhappy children were treated tenderly and lovingly, gently wooed back into the classroom community. Classroom rules such as "We will love and respect each other" reflect the theme of building a caring community. The schoolwide focus on the golden rule—"Do unto others as you would have them do unto you"—also supports the goal of caring for and about one another.

Care and support of children as they become readers is evident in Teresa's classroom, as she gently coaxes them to talk about their weekend reading. When their individual needs and problems are expressed (fights among family members, spending the weekend with another parent, personal and financial crises, worries and fears), Teresa helps them to problem solve ways to find a time and place to read. Trust is vital in this classroom community if students are to risk sharing their personal struggles.

Mutual love and respect between teacher and students and between teacher and parents is evident in outward expressions of affection as well as in the quality of listening and sharing. Before class I noticed many hugs, warm smiles, and compliments—a kind word about Tiara's new coat or George's baby sister. A girl who was in tears yesterday, upset about her grandmother, is asked by her teacher, "How are you feeling?" And before breakfast each morning the children say in chorus, "It's nice to have breakfast with our friends." They are learning in many small ways to appreciate each other and to support the value of each member of their classroom family.

Evelyn's mother sent an apologetic note to her teacher for not helping Evelyn with homework; she had to take one of her young twins to the hospital. Likewise, another mother felt comfortable enough with the teacher to request that any leftover milk be sent home for their new baby—a good example of the trust level present in the parent-teacher relationship.

In the hallway, Miguel's dad told his son's teacher about the problem he had getting into the building to do some volunteer work at the school. Those at the front door wouldn't let him in, telling him he had to walk around to the back of the building. The teacher listened respectfully, then said she would bring the issue up at the next faculty meeting, "Because we're trying to get parents to come into the school, and yet they're discouraging you."

Valuing, appreciating, and supporting students is demonstrated in Debby Perry's first-grade classroom when a student has difficulty with reading. Debby's students come to the front of the room and read their chosen books into a microphone, as a class performance. Debby is enthusiastically supportive and encouraging when one student has trouble with *Bears* (a nonfiction book). Debby says, "This book is not meant to be read by first graders. If you want a really, really hard book to read, this is the book for you!"

When another student, Juan, chooses a new book to read, Debby says, "Wow! This is a new book—are you sure you want to do this?" She has to lower the microphone to accommodate his height, and the class laughs. So she says, "Hey! I'd rather be short and smart." Then she adds, to Juan, "And you *are* smart."

In Maggie Smith's first-grade classroom she is patiently respectful with some very active students, gives many reminders and explanations about their behavior, and involves them in thinking and talking about how they could have done things differently when things do not go smoothly:

Maggie: What do you think we could have done differently?
Phillip: We were talking.
Maggie: Talking is fine, but we also need to listen and learn.
Francisco: We should have the lights out.
Anthony: We should have whispered.

The Class Rules list and discipline calendar used in Teresa's classroom illustrate the theme of building respectful and trusting relationships, and partnering with parents in support of the children. Some of the class rules are:

> We must love and respect each other.
>
> We must be nice to and respect everyone who enters our classroom.
>
> We must listen and pay attention.
>
> When someone is talking or sharing, we must be quiet and give them the attention and respect they deserve.
>
> We must try our very best.
>
> We will not give up easily or get frustrated. We may not say, "I can't do this; I don't want to do this." We must try.
>
> We will ask questions.
>
> If we do not understand what is being said or taught, we must ask the teacher to explain it.

The Class Rules list and discipline calendar went home to the parents, and included items individual children needed help with (such as not hurting other's feelings, being prepared for class, and so on), and parents wrote back to express their concerns and talked with Teresa about particular behavior issues. She notes that the parents were helping the children with behavior at home. Teresa ends the day by sitting with her class in a circle and talking about the good things she noticed them doing during the day (she takes notes on this to share with them).

Collaborative teacher-to-teacher relationships at Taylor also work to help children with difficulties in the classroom. During the SLC work sampling meeting, Pat Kelly talked about a disruptive child whose behavior was getting worse. There was a twenty-minute presentation and discussion of the student, not unlike Pat Carini's (1996) "staff review of a child." The discussion was mediated at times by Jorge, a family therapist from the University of Pennsylvania's Child Guidance Clinic, and the principal, Wendy Shapiro, who offered helpful suggestions and encouragement.

Pat was supported and encouraged in her efforts, and teachers asked questions to help her think of other possibilities for looking at the strengths of the child. This was followed by positive suggestions from the group for working with the child. Jorge asked what Pat had been doing that was working well, and he said it was remarkable that the child was doing as well as he was, given all the difficulties he faced. The entire session was supportive of Pat, so that she could, in turn, support the child.

Earlier SLC meetings illustrated the same helpful, respectful, supportive relationships among the teachers. The meetings were positive problem-solving experiences as well as opportunities to share ideas and get support from colleagues. My notes and reflections on several of the meetings illustrate that there was an attitude of understanding and patience with regard to new members, a "We can do this" approach to problem solving, collegiality, and respect for each other's questions, problems, and issues, and a positive attitude toward the possibilities for change.

On the theme of support for children with family crises, second grader Ciara said that the after-school dance club (led by Debby Perry) helps her when things are bad at home and mom and dad are fighting. Earlier in class, Teresa suggested that Ciara take a book and go read somewhere when her parents fight. Both teachers are there for Ciara to hear her problems, care about her, and support her in finding ways to deal with tough situations.

Relationships with the Community

In an after-school EPOP meeting with several teachers and parents, Gordon Whitman, Wendy Shapiro, Gina Kaplan, Julia Sanabria, and parent leader Ortencia Santiago explained that the purpose of EPOP was to build relationships, not lay blame, to work together toward needed changes, not accept excuses. And, in fact, as collaborating parents, teachers, and administrators, they worked together respectfully and successfully on the lunch and breakfast program improvements, the book-reading program, gathering information on the Reading

Recovery program, and in developing a Library Power initiative in the school.

Empowerment of parents, respect across race and class, and collaboration between the school and community was evident at a 2 P.M. professional development meeting in the spring, in which the faculty supported the EPOP parent-reading initiatives. Gina, Wendy, and Debby Perry clarified and supported the parent-reading-program ideas. Gina explained that parents will do the paperwork, and Wendy discussed the twelve-week goal of twelve books for third and fourth graders and twenty books for first and second graders. Wendy also stressed the need for more experiences with reading, and she said that books could and should be taken home, even if they are lost (addressing one teacher's fear of losing her classroom books).

At an earlier professional development meeting Wendy talked with teachers about the difficulty of talking about race, but she said she wants to start a conversation around Peggy McIntosh's (1989) article "White Privilege," which she gave to the entire faculty to read. She assured the faculty that as a community they can talk about this issue, suggesting the trusting, mutually respectful relationship they have built together.

During the October Back to School Night, parents were welcomed warmly and respectfully by Wendy in both Spanish and English. She went beyond merely inviting the parents in, asking them to "please" come in to help at the school, expressing to them how very much they are needed and wanted.

Parents are welcomed into the classroom and serve as helpers as well as visitors. Georgio's dad helps with breakfast. Bianco's mom stays until 10:30 A.M. to help. Francisco's mom comes into the classroom to hear of his good behavior and to see the butterfly and larva. Another parent brings a turtle in for the class. Both Maggie and Teresa suggested including classroom assistants (some of whom are parents) in the SLC meetings and having assistants make observations of the students as well.

On support and caring for families/mothers in crisis, Nydia (the bilingual counselor assistant) told me about a mother who came into the school in tears, suffering from abuse. The school staff found her a shelter away from the area and gave her bus money to get there. Evelyn Alicea, the school-community coordinator, visits homes and is a support to families in the community. She connects families with a number of agencies and services, such as Centro Pedro Claver, ASPIRA, Association of Puerto Ricans on the March (APM), Congreso de

Latinos Unidos, Casa del Carmen, Taller Puertorriqueño Community Center, and the Lighthouse.

Additional support for families in crisis comes from Southern Homes Services, which provides four social workers at Taylor and an after-school homework club on Tuesday and Thursday. The director, Carmen Quirindongo, explained that her bilingual social workers can make home visits, observe and work with teachers in the classroom, make assessments, prepare a family service plan, and prepare a contract with the family concerning their goals and needs. They also help to connect families with other agencies and services in the community.

Although there are many differences among the teachers concerning teaching philosophy and methods, the staff is able to work together, care for, and support one another, appreciate and celebrate one another, and respect one another. One example of this is the large-family dining-room-table atmosphere in the faculty and staff lunchroom. Often teachers, assistants, and other staff members bring food to share at lunchtime, and the conversations flow back and forth easily from the personal to the professional.

Supportive relationships at Taylor have developed and are sustained because of:

1. the family environment that has been created through the daily faculty lunchroom time (which the principal and support staff as well as parent/classroom assistants participate in)
2. the biweekly two-hour professional development meetings, to discuss and develop curriculum, talk about philosophy and evaluation, and problem solve
3. a history of being a schoolwide project school with adequate funding to do what is collaboratively planned
4. democratic, supportive, problem-solving, advocacy-oriented, bilingual principals over the past five years
5. faculty trips to New York City, coalition retreats/workshops, plays, conferences
6. spaghetti dinners and other school functions that the staff plan together as colleagues and friends
7. a schoolwide focus on what is best for the children
8. the fact that members of the school work hard, celebrate each other's successes, and feel that they are a family—the Taylor Family

Orchestration of the Learning Process

Ongoing professional development and what Ladson-Billings (1994) describes as culturally responsive teaching are, of course, vital for a successful school. Diana Diaz and Teresa Alvarez's thematic units on Puerto Rico, and the centers they have in their classrooms, filled with artifacts from Puerto Rico, Nicaragua, and the Dominican Republic, are good examples of this.

Debby Williams' first/second nongraded classroom provides excellent examples of teaching for independence and empowerment, giving personal choices, and supporting the growth of her students. The books in the literature-study groups are chosen by students, and they make their own list of words they have trouble with, including flash cards they take home.

Debby moves around the classroom to each group of students and coaches enthusiastically: "Very good! Give her a hand!" She mediates in their thinking, urging them ahead to fuller explanations and interpretations of the literature: "Can you tell me more?" "Why would you think that?" Debby will sometimes stop to coach on errors, but not on all of them, and never intrusively in a "checking up on you" style. She strives to find the teachable moment—a mediation or facilitation move like, "Notice where the period is."

The challenging vocabulary on the blackboard word list includes *Precambrian, Paleozoic, Cenozoic, Triassic, amphibians, extinct, erupt, lava, fossils, millions*. Content is challenging, interesting, and motivating, and her students rise to her high expectations. Some of the sentences underneath the list are (1) During the Triassic period the continents were together. It was very hot. (2) Then the continents began to separate. (3) Finally the dinosaurs could no longer live.

Debby Perry's first graders do an enthusiastic rap on the planets, the oceans, and the continents with great rhythm, engagement, and fun. Then she sets up a microphone and speakers so that each student can read orally a selection they have practiced from their own little library of take-home books. This group of thematic books is about bears: *Brown Bear, Brown Bear; Everywhere Bears; Bear Sleeps in Winter; All About Bears*. Debby announces that today is a practice reading for a read-aloud evaluation. Students come to the microphone and read with enthusiasm, students applaud, and Debby shakes their hand in congratulations.

A good example of teaching for change and growth is Teresa's second-grade curriculum for transformation that is linked with the personal interests of the students. A morning language arts lesson *If I Could* features a story about what one could be in the future, which describes possible professions: a firefighter to save lives, a librarian, tour guide, pilot, scientist, et cetera.

After the story sharing, Teresa asks students to close their eyes and imagine what they are going to be. As they share their dreams of becoming a dentist, teacher, hairdresser, police officer, football player, and so on, Teresa encourages them to think positively of what they *will* be and what they are *going* to be—not just what they hope or wish to be.

Her empowerment teaching, like Debbie Williams' song lyrics at Harrington ("I Believe I Can Fly"), stresses dreaming large dreams and then becoming what you dream: If they can see it, they can do it. And if they believe it, there's nothing to it. Teresa says that Kimberly knows she is going to be a dentist and that nothing is going to stop her. Tara wants to be a teacher, and her mother tells me that she plays the role of teacher at home with friends.

In Diana Diaz's third-fourth-grade bilingual class there is laughter and fun as they sing the song from the book *Follow the Drinking Gourd*, with Amy, a very active and vocal girl, taking the lead. Diana allows much risk taking and experimenting, making all students feel that they are part of the classroom family. Diana explained to me that Amy had been failing in an English-instruction classroom, despite the fact that she is very bright. To support her confidence, Diana lets Amy take some leadership roles. To encourage her students to include Amy, Diana says, "We don't want to be rude to Amy. She's our classmate."

Taylor is organized in various ways for reflection on teaching, learning, and staff collaboration. The Tuesday afternoon staff development sessions provide many opportunities to work on issues of curriculum, relationships, and school environment. The time is built into the schedule, and children go home early so that all teachers can participate. SLC meetings are scheduled each week and built into the regular day's schedule. Pat, Maggie, and Teresa's time is at 9:30 A.M. every Friday. This provides weekly opportunities to share ideas, resources, questions, and problems as well as time for reflection on their focus, work sampling.

And what do the students say about their own learning? When one teacher asked her second-grade students what teachers do to make them better readers, they responded:

They read to us and we read to them.

Teachers tell you to practice.

They say to take a book and read it.

You give us a book and we go home and read it with our mom.

[You tell us to] eat breakfast and drink orange juice and it will make you strong so you can learn.

Student experiences of reading include meaningful and authentic reading between teachers and students, students and parents, and students and peers. In reference to the motivating environment for learning, the value students place on reading, and the empowering metaphors that they have learned from their teacher, students say (about learning to read) that:

Reading makes you smarter.

Reading is the ticket to go to college.

When you plant a seed, the seed starts to grow.

Your brains grow.

You start learning new stuff.

The Importance of Funding

Equally important in the success of both Taylor and Harrington schools is the issue of adequate material resources. These are underfunded public city schools in very poor neighborhoods, but people within them have been successful in finding scarce resources for their efforts.

A not-to-be-discounted cause for the success of these schools is the district schoolwide project money and grants from foundations and other sources. Taylor and Harrington each received six hundred thousand dollars in 1989 from the schoolwide project initiative. And both schools have received money through the Philadelphia Education Fund and through other sources for a variety of school initiatives such as Library Power and Arts Empower at Harrington.

This is not to say that they do not need more funding. There is often no toilet paper, no soap, and no hand towels in the bathrooms; and there is never enough money for better classroom libraries, sets of good children's books, math manipulatives, computers, science equipment, and other much-needed supplies.

It is also not to say that other urban schools are therefore able to do the same thing as Taylor and Harrington, whose stable faculties have worked collaboratively over a number of years, using each other as resources, and who have learned to successfully connect with out-side agencies for much-needed funding.

The bottom line is, there is not enough money available from private foundations, special grants, or city school districts for all urban schools to be equitably supported. Private and local efforts can never make up for the grossly inequitable system of public school funding, based on local property taxes, that presently exists. There is a direct parallel here with social welfare funding: food banks, shelters, churches, and private charities cannot make up for the erosion of the vitally needed safety net for poor children and their families.

Large-scale transformational change, rooted in a democratic commitment to the common good and to equality of educational op-portunity for all children, is a subject to which we will return in Chap-ter 7. Such change will demand knowledgeable leadership, creativity, commitment, and deeper understanding from policymakers, along with a better-informed general public to advocate for change.

PART II: A CLOSER LOOK AT TAYLOR

I Can Send My Own Child Here

In one of our interviews, Teresa told me the story of her first faculty meeting at Taylor. Someone remarked that there was no use beginning a new program at the school, because "these" children couldn't learn, and Teresa felt compelled to share what she believed about the learn-ing abilities of all children. I quote her at length here because this is such a good example of the influence of a committed parent and teacher who brings her knowledge of the community into the school as a force for change.

> Teresa, 10/2/96
>
> When I came here nine years ago, there was a faculty meeting, and it was at the time when schoolwide projects were being of-fered to the school. At that time our principal was trying, along with an outside person, to present the staff with a schoolwide project proposal that would bring money and opportunities into the school.
>
> And a colleague had stated that it was, I guess in her own words, sort of like a waste of money and a waste of time, because *these* children came from a neighborhood that could not provide

them with whatever knowledge or resources they would need to make use of what was going to be provided by the program.

It really upset me, because I was sitting in the audience thinking, first of all, I had not been officially introduced to the staff—it was my first week here. And it upset me to think that I live in the neighborhood, my children live in the neighborhood. This would be the neighborhood school my own children would attend. And if I was to place my child in the building with this kind of mentality going on through the staff, then the child was not going to be successful—because he would be coming into a classroom where the teacher thought that way. So my child's going to eventually start thinking the same way.

I raised my hand and I asked for my turn to speak, and I stated the fact that I was very upset (I mean, [by] my face, you could tell that I was very upset). And I said, "Don't you dare tell me that my children cannot learn in this environment! I live in this community. The children that go to Saint Veronica's, the Catholic sister school to Taylor, are from the same neighborhood that these children at Taylor are coming from. The same resources, the same type of living environment. And if they can do it, there's no reason why children at Taylor cannot do it, if *we* provide the motivation for them to be here."

That was, I guess, the start of my looking at Taylor school as the place where my own children would want to go. I remember the principal (I can't remember if it was at that same meeting or later on)—he had approached me earlier to share my motivation, my enthusiasm for teaching, with the staff, and I did. And I stated the fact that most of these children can learn, will learn, if we provide for them.

And some of them, all they needed was, you know, [a] "You can do it!" And a hug once in a while. And that's my way of showing children that I care about them. And if other teachers could do the same thing—and I'm not saying that all the teachers don't—but in general, you can see that if everyone cared, the children would start caring too about their own education. And that's how that came about.

And eventually we did say at the meeting that if we could make Taylor school a school where our own children would be able to attend, and that we would *want* our children to attend, then we've accomplished what we want to do with this school.

Teresa's strong advocacy for the children in the community and their potential was underscored by the fact that she was raising her own children in the community. She suggested that, if a teacher would not want to send her own children to the school where she taught, there was something wrong that needed to be looked at carefully and fixed. Two years later she felt that the school had improved enough to send her own child there. Teresa's advocacy for the children of the community, her own commitment to teaching and learning, her model of rapport with and support of the families in the community, and her enthusiastic collaboration with her colleagues at the school played no small part in the transformation of the school.

We Hug Here

From observations on the playground, walking the hallways, and in the classroom, I noticed that "We hug here." This extended to the principal, the teachers, the parents, and the students. One example that stands out for me is of two little African American girls, seven and eight years old, who I called "the crying sisters" in my notes. When they arrived at Taylor for the first time, they looked lost, afraid, and very sad. And they cried that entire first day.

They were eventually wooed into the classroom community with many hugs and an enveloping warmth that they could not resist. Frequently throughout the first several days of their attendance, the teacher had one little girl under each arm, or sitting on her lap, or holding her hand, as she taught. When I asked about the crying sisters a month later, the response was, "They love it here!"

Another example is from Maggie Smith's first-grade classroom. When I arrived in her classroom the first time, I saw her sitting on the floor with her arms around three or four of her first graders. Maggie worked very hard and very patiently to show her students the concern and respect that she wanted them to share with one another. And it worked, as is evidenced from the following:

> Fieldwork journal, 2/25/97
>
> Just came from Maggie's classroom, where her first graders were so quietly respectful during the circle discussion she was having from 10:30 to 11:00 A.M. They shared time to talk individually, they were quiet when they needed to be, and they sat in the circle for a long time, participating in interactive dialogue with her on several topics. There were only minimal periods of too much over-

lapping speech (within a one-person-at-a-time-speaks model) where Maggie had to pause, ask for respect, and ask individuals by name to control their own behavior. Only Phillip had to go back to his seat, and he was not disruptive there, still engaged in the discussion of *Beauty and the Beast*, and still wanting to answer Maggie's questions about the meaning of the story.

Professional Development

Schoolwide project work was started before the Coalition of Essential Schools (Sizer 1997) membership, and this had the greatest impact on teacher professional development, according to Teresa. This unprecedented offer of six hundred thousand dollars from the school district encouraged teachers to begin working together to develop thematic units and to attend seminars and workshops with the stipulation that they would come back to teach their peers. They were to present to their fellow professionals in faculty meetings and professional development meetings at their schools. This grassroots development plan allowed for individual choice, interests, and freedom to learn. There was a rich diversity in the interests, but there was also the checks-and-balances system of teachers talking with the principal and colleagues about (1) why they wanted to attend a given conference/workshop/seminar, and (2) how this related to the school's overall goals.

Faculty members at Taylor collaborate around a common framework and are responsible for their own development and growth. This framework unifies the school amid grassroots diversity: We celebrate diversity here; we provide choices here; we encourage teachers to follow their interests. And all of this provides a model for what can and does happen in the classroom, with respect to student's ideas, interests, diversity, and choices, as well as what happens in interaction with parents and the community.

There is a schoolwide focus on respect for others as exemplified by the golden rule: "Do unto others as you would have them do unto you." This corresponds with one of the coalition's principles: a tone of decency throughout the school. Gina Kaplan, the program support teacher, explained that professional development with respect to the coalition principles comes from a variety of teachers and administrators—whoever is available to go to a given conference or workshop. They bring back the ideas to the faculty, and ways to extend them are developed in collaboration with the faculty. The coalition provides a way to look at school reform and cluster with other schools in the city

(McClure Elementary and Roberto Clemente Middle School) and across the country (Sizer 1997).

Small learning communities (SLCs) provide another opportunity for continual, collaborative professional development. Teresa and Maggie's SLC does work sampling, and they attend professional development opportunities related to observing children's work and doing alternative assessment. A nongraded SLC, which includes Debby Williams, developed a narrative report card with a checklist for evaluation. Other teachers have participated in the Penn Literacy Network and Penn Writing Project, and they have brought student-centered language-learning ideas to the school, which are rooted in the Pennsylvania Framework for Reading, Writing, and Talking Across the K–12 Curriculum (Lytle and Botel 1991).

A Marriage of Knowledge and Care

Learning to care, as well as learning to know, was a part of many Taylor faculty meetings that I attended. An after-school professional development meeting held in the spring serves to illustrate this dual purpose. Two teachers who had attended a standards workshop (Brenda Mitchell and Lillian Tearte) presented for an hour to the faculty on assessment principles. The teachers did a very professional job of presenting, the faculty was engaged and interested, and the concluding discussion about assessment principles was both passionate and thoughtful, while also being respectful.

Then the speech teacher, Juanita Leysath, did a brief "imagining" exercise about living in the community and experiencing what the children experience on a daily basis. The faculty was asked to close their eyes as she read the following scenarios.

> You are leaving Taylor School and going home for the day. You are not driving away in your cars; rather, you are walking home as a Taylor student. You walk past the graffiti-covered walls, over the broken glass, and over the drug paraphernalia that litters the streets. You arrive at your house and go in. On the table is a note from your mother. It reads, "Maria, yo fui a la tienda. Empieza las assignaciones. Mami." (Maria, I went to the store. Start your homework. Mommy.)
>
> You sit back and reflect on your day at school. It was Career Day and your assignment is to write about which speaker you enjoyed the most. You decide to write about Sra. Melendez, the

attorney. You remember how she reminded you of your Aunt Teresa. Sra. Melendez spoke about attending ESOL classes when she attended school, and also of her friends dropping out or having babies. She said that she had been determined to go on and she was the first high school graduate in her family. She went to college where she never had any Latino professors and had very few Latino friends. She continued on to attend law school and is now a successful attorney. You decide that you also want to beat the statistics of 50 percent of Latinos dropping out of high school, and you want to attend college.

You are a young boy walking home, Rasheed. You also walk over the glass and drug-related litter to your home. When you go inside there is a letter waiting for you. It reads, "Rasheed, I had to take your little sister to the doctor. Start your homework. Grandmom."

You also have to write about Career Day, and you decide to write about Mr. Johnson, the McDonald's franchise owner. Mr. Johnson said that while growing up he attended Philadelphia public schools and never thought that some day he would be a McDonald's owner. He studied hard, went to school when friends might have been cutting classes, and worked hard. He went to college and worked his way up to different positions. Then he was sent to a special training program where he was one of only two African Americans in the program. You also want to be successful.

When the homework is finished, you turn on the TV as the evening news is about to come on. You see the top stories are, once again, killings, drug busts, and violence in neighborhoods that look like yours.

This professional development meeting illustrates some of the ways that Taylor continues to evolve as both a caring and knowledgeable faculty. Because the faculty is equally committed to their own professional development and to the lives of their students, the agenda for these meetings often includes curriculum and evaluation issues along with ways to better understand, support, empathasize with, and care for the children in the school.

The Trust Issue

Trust is a vital part of the Taylor family. People trust the sincerity and commitment of one another. Teresa feels that way about Wendy, trusting that Wendy tried as hard as she could to not take her out of her classroom at a critical time of the year when another bilingual teacher took a position at the cluster office. Even disaffected or seemingly less invested teachers do not try to sabotage the program/school/each other, instead sharing respect and favorable comments about other teachers.

There is much internal cheerleading as well as external promoting of the school. Sue Kettell, the physical education teacher, promoted the school to the Children Achieving office, and Corina Wong came to visit, writing a highly complimentary letter to Wendy, which Wendy then shared with the teachers.

The EPOP meeting was a good example of trust, respect, and open dialogue among parents, teachers, and administration. Ortencia, a strong parent leader, felt free to push for a better reading program; the teachers felt free to offer their advice and suggestions; and Wendy and Gina were open about the issues that were involved.

Wendy openly shared knowledgeable information about the reading-program ideas, saying she would look into various aspects of the proposed program. Ortencia introduced a twelve-week book-reading initiative, and shared information about both the Reading Recovery program and the Library Power model, all of which were received with interest and enthusiasm by the faculty. They made plans to include parents in the site visits to look at these models in other schools.

There was no hostility, tension, or aversive interaction during the meetings that I attended, nor any others that I heard about. Parents and staff appeared to trust the good intentions of each other, and they later told me that they felt they were all working toward what is best for the children.

The School as a Family System

"We are family" stands out to me as I think about Taylor: an open, supportive, developing family. In family-systems (Napier and Whitaker 1978) terms, it is an interactive and functional family that does not hold family secrets and silence members, does not scapegoat and blame members, but instead cares for and supports all of its members. This family system is open to learning and to the optimal development of each human being—teachers as well as students and parents.

This open family system (Minuchin 1974) strives to make sense, make meaning, learn, and grow. Individual members have personal choice and freedom, and they also have personal responsibility for themselves and for each other. It is a mutually supportive and interdependent system, whose social interactions build upon each other so that growth and learning are the outcomes.

The potential of individual members can be realized in this open family system, while at the same time there is support for the continuation and sustenance of the family as a whole. Life makes sense and has meaning and purpose in this system. Activities are designed for authentic/real learning, and they make inherent sense to the students as well as the teachers and parents.

Family relationships are open, respectful, and mutually supportive. Even potentially divisive issues such as race can be put on the table. There is open communication in a trust-filled, risk-free environment that allows people to say what they think and feel, and to build deeper and richer relationships with one another. Family members genuinely care about each other, support each other, and feed/sustain each other in a variety of ways.

Physically, they are concerned for each other's health, sustenance, and well-being. The faculty lunchroom is often the center of this nurturance—much like the family kitchen table. People congregate here, share lunch and snack foods with each other, and enjoy family dinner table conversation. Teachers, administrators, other staff, and parent aides all come together in the faculty lunchroom before, during, and after school.

Emotionally, the faculty demonstrates care and concern for one another's personal needs. Personal and family difficulties as well as celebrations are shared throughout the school. Plans for Maggie's wedding, Diana's mother's illness and death, concern for a teacher's daughter, and the death of a spouse—all are shared and supported by the Taylor family.

Cognitively, family members support each other's learning and growth. There is much sharing of teaching methods, teaching resources, and ideas. Teachers call each other after school to ask for help or to share ideas. When I was staying with Teresa, a fellow teacher called her in the evening with questions about an approach to math. Teresa shared ideas and invited her to visit her classroom to observe her practice.

Spiritually, the Taylor family encourages hopefulness and keeping the faith. The Taylor motto is Yes I can! and that spirit is pervasive for both teachers and students. There is a mutually supportive environment that teachers, administrators, social workers, senior citizen

"Experience Corps" volunteers, and other support staff work very hard to create.

Evidence that the faculty is functioning well as opposed to merely functioning comes from the many less successful urban elementary schools that are closed family systems. They do not support and sustain each other. They have made scapegoats of teachers, principals, students, or families. They have silenced their members. Many fear open communication about race, culture, and language. And many do not support the ongoing growth and learning of all members.

Giving the current educational system a failing grade, Sarason (1999) describes an effective system as a "coordinated, non-adversarial, self-correcting arrangement of parts" (163). The Taylor school system operates successfully, according to this definition: a good model for the rest of the educational system, which includes colleges, universities, state departments of education, national and state legislators and executives, and boards of education.

Teresa's personal oasis, her own home in the community, parallels the school in its spirit of hopefulness and persistence in the midst of gunshots, traffic, drugs and crime, poverty, and societal neglect. But why should she and the school have to do this in spite of, rather than in addition to, other larger social, political, and economic efforts to support urban families and children?

Family Life

I asked Teresa if I could live with her for a few weeks to better understand the perspective of parents and community members, and she was kind enough to let me share her daughter Teresita's room. The following journal entries and analytic memos are from my visit at Teresa's home in North Philadelphia, four blocks from the Taylor school.

(2/24/97)

This morning at Teresa's home we talked about the school breakfast program. Teresa said that she has breakfast for her class in her room because there were too many children who didn't come to school on time to get it in the school cafeteria before 8:30 A.M. They have to meet their teacher on the playground at 8:40 to come to class, so getting to school on time for breakfast would mean coming to school a half hour earlier.

Other children who are not in her class also come into her room for breakfast. She takes it as her responsibility to make sure that all of her children get their breakfast, so she has chosen to take the extra ten minutes for this in her room at 9 A.M. The kindergarten teachers also have breakfast in the room for the students.

Some teachers have said that it should be more the parents' responsibility to be sure that the children are at school on time for the free breakfast at 8 A.M. They feel that, since they too had once been poor and had managed to work their way up to being a teacher, there is no excuse for parents not doing the same.

I shared Teresa's discouragement with the "pull yourself up by your own bootstraps" mentality when things are *not* the same with parents today. There is more racism and prejudice, less support for families and children (especially if your mother tongue is other than English), more entrenched and seemingly intractable drug, crime, housing, and employment problems, and a mean-spirited political climate that values property rights and monetary worth over human rights, human worth, and the common good.

(2/27/97)

Teresa and I talked about the loud noise outside on the street and all of the drive-by drug action on the corner, two doors up from Teresa's house. They are selling crack cocaine, and dealers came to my car window each time I pulled up to find a parking place outside Teresa's home. She told me that a few years ago, when she had organized a drug march in the neighborhood, her front windows were broken out afterward and she was very frightened. Teresa asked me if I heard the gunshots at night, because they happen every night as cars drive by and the drug traffic continues until early in the morning. Two doors up there are young men on the corners all night selling drugs.

When I arrived in North Philadelphia to stay with Teresa and her family, I was driving around the block in search of Teresa's house on Sunday night when a young man came up to my car window asking something I didn't understand. Teresa and Edgardo explained later that he was asking if I wanted drugs. Not knowing why he came over, I naively asked him to help me find Teresa's house—which he did.

On Monday night, as we returned from a parent-teacher conference and looked in vain for a parking place, Teresa said she knew the young man who was on the corner. His father had died several years before, she told me, and he became involved in drugs. His mother was helping him to get out, but then his mother also died, and he is all alone.

So he is out on the street. Another victim of a society that isn't organized sufficiently to prevent tragedies when its young people are caught in a failure cycle: when they drop out of school, become orphans, and have no healthy life supports. It is the criminal justice system that is being funded to deal with these young people, which is why we have the highest incarceration rate of any country in the world, alongside the highest child poverty rate in the industrialized world.

With no job, little hope, and few opportunities, a job on the street becomes attractive to young people because of the easy money. Eventually, they can more easily become addicted and start using what they are selling.

Teresa told me about others she knew who dropped out of high school and later became addicted to heroin. Part of the problem is the lessons learned in the schools, which are microcosms of the larger society and reflect its attitudes: you are not competent; you are stupid; you cannot succeed; we do not expect much from you; you are not one of "us": you are one of "them"; you do not have a culture and a history (that the school and teachers understand and respect and celebrate).

Part of the problem is the racism and prejudice in the society that young people face in their communities as they try to get jobs and a place to live:

1. prejudice against Spanish-speaking people—a senseless bias that refuses to celebrate bilingualism as a gift and a resource

2. prejudice against immigrant families who are following in the footsteps and tradition of the predecessors of most U.S. citizens who sought a better life for themselves and their families

3. prejudice and ignorance about the status of Puerto Ricans, who are, in fact, U.S. citizens, having had Commonwealth status since 1952

4. prejudice and fear of low-income families, assumed to be "welfare leeches," when the reality is that over 25 percent of eligible Spanish-speaking families get no welfare benefits because of their limited English and subsequent inability to make it through the maze of bureaucratic paperwork, for which there are few resources to advise and assist

The Wider Ecology

The impossibility of living on the meager welfare benefits provided for families suffering from loss of jobs, lack of adequate education or housing, and no health care is illustrated well in *Myth of the Welfare Queen* by David Zucchino (1997), *Tyranny of Kindness* by Theresa Funiciello (1993), and *So You Think I Drive a Cadillac?* by Karen Seccome (1999). This impossibility is faced by poor city parents and children in the midst of "reform" politics and mandates that continually attack the integrity of poor families, crudely invade their privacy, cruelly criticize and blame them for their own nearly insurmountable problems, and offer little hope or support for their future (Polakow 2000).

Recently a family with a child who had suffered severe asthma attacks came to Teresa for help. They had just moved to the neighborhood, and the parents, grandparents, and two children were living in a damp, mildew-filled basement. Teresa managed to link them with a local housing agency, Centro Pedro Claver, and they found a more livable place for their child. Similarly, she has advised other families about what to do when the electricity, heat, or water is turned off in their homes.

Welfare "reforms" have only added to the problem, eliminating for many poor families what was only a marginal safety net. In North Philadelphia, the Kensington Welfare Rights Union (see www.kwru.org) has been documenting many of these economic human rights abuses, both in North Philadelphia and across the United States. KWRU works at a grassroots level to help homeless and poor people organize and support each other. Cheri Honkala has led the organization to work on both the local realities and the larger issues. They have taken over abandoned HUD houses to give homeless families a place to live, and they have also organized marches and demonstrations to build a larger national movement to end poverty and homelessness.

There is also the larger context of a "justice" system that disproportionately incarcerates Latino and African American men. David Cole's *No Equal Justice* (1999) and Bill Ayers' *A Kind and Just Parent* (1998) document this alarming, ongoing injustice and inequality, as does the *Phi Delta Kappan* special report (October 1997) on "African American Males and the Criminal Justice System." This same justice system "ignores" or is slow to come to the aid of citizens in poor urban communities. Teresa told me the story of how she had made an urgent call to the police when her son Miguel, then a young child, was missing, their delay in responding, and their refusal, once there, to come into her home to talk with her, due to their fear and prejudice.

REFLECTION: WHAT STOOD OUT FOR ME

☐ The school community at Taylor benefits from the celebration of the language and culture of the families.

☐ Taylor's observation-based evaluation contributes to a learning environment of warmth, support, and care.

☐ Strong parent leadership and collaboration with teachers builds relationships rooted in trust and respect.

☐ Professional development that is both individual and collaborative supports both knowledge and colleagueship.

☐ Schools that are open family systems continue to learn and grow in collaboration with students and families.

☐ Challenges are presented to schools by the child and family welfare system, the juvenile/criminal justice system, and the political system, which are failing poor urban children and their families.

4

Teaching and Learning at Harrington
"Doing the Right Thing"

Harrington Elementary School is located at Baltimore Avenue and 53rd Street in West Philadelphia in a low-income, predominately African American community. Of the eight hundred students in the school, 98 percent are African American. The large old school building is kept in good repair, and the inside entrance to the school is invitingly decorated with student artwork.

There was graffiti on the lower levels of the school when I came to observe in September, but this was gone by the time I had returned for two weeks in October. As I walked outside around the school building in September, I watched with much curiosity an older woman who was picking up trash around the school. When I asked her what she was doing, she explained that she was part of a group of community members who make themselves available to paint over graffiti and pick up litter around the building. They do this to show the children that people in the community care about them and their school.

Later, one spring afternoon as I was sitting on the front steps of the school admiring the beautiful white flowering trees, a crossing guard told me that the trees were a gift from a previous kindergarten teacher at the school, who is now retired. I was told later by Barbara Davies that this teacher was part of a beautification project, and that she helped write a grant proposal for a project connected with the Horticulture Society of Philadelphia. Her students sold plants and the money collected went toward purchasing the trees.

PART I: THE ECOLOGY OF HARRINGTON

An Overview of Harrington

Two special programs at the school—Arts Empower and Library Power—are an aesthetic delight at Harrington. The success of the Arts Empower program is evident in the beautiful student artwork throughout the building, including in the entrance, hallways, and classrooms. This program, supported by teacher-written grants and funded by the William Penn Foundation, stands out as student-centered and visually inviting. Under the leadership of Rosa Serota, the art teacher, it is philosophically grounded in integrated, experiential, artistic learning.

The Library Power program, funded through the Dewitt Wallace Foundation and administered through the Philadelphia Education Fund, is both a philosophy and a well-designed library. Under the direction of librarian Renee Stroback, the library has inviting areas for a variety of projects and activities, run for and by students, with teachers available as resources and coaches. Students can come to the library whenever they want a book—just like they would use the public library. And they check out their own books, assisted by older students, and use their own personal library card. It was amazing to observe little first graders using this process so responsibly.

In the classrooms, there is much emphasis on reading to and with the students, providing opportunities to write, and doing much low-risk choral and oral reading practice in groups. One classroom has a predominance of opportunities to write, with continual student monitoring and coaching (miniconferences every day for every child). Another classroom has a predominance of opportunities to read, with choral and echo reading, as well as independent reading, followed by oral reading to and by an adult throughout the day. The influence of Carol Hirschfeld's twenty-eight years of language arts facilitating and mentoring is evident.

Continual teacher monitoring of homework and class work is common in the classrooms in which I observed. Students are held accountable for doing their "job" (their schoolwork), and for "doing the right thing" (the school motto), and for taking responsibility for their own learning and behavior. This extends to the library as well, with its student-run checkout system and independent visits for all grades. There are no assigned whole-class visits to the library.

Parents and administrators feel that the faculty is the real strength of the school. They view the faculty as open to parents, hardworking, caring, and committed. Many faculty members have been at the school for ten, twenty, or more years, and some are teaching the children of their previous students.

Past and present principals at Harrington have emphasized welcoming the parents into the school and into the classroom. Some teachers also have grandparents in their classrooms as volunteers or as chaperones on field trips. Administrators encourage teachers to answer parents' questions, to be willing to solve problems when they come up, to focus on the positives in interaction with parents, and to be generally supportive of parents. According to parent reports, this seems to be working. I observed many parents coming in to talk with teachers, to back up teachers when students are not doing the right thing, and to help out in the classroom.

The Teachers

Teachers demand the full attention of students in the classroom at Harrington. They also insist on having homework done, on full participation in classroom activities, and on student responsibility. The school is regarded by the former students, parents, new teachers, and substitute teachers with whom I talked as having well-behaved children.

The teachers are also advocates for their students. They speak up in faculty meetings against the standardized testing of children, which they insist leaves their students feeling frustrated, angry, and discouraged. They believe that in many cases the tests are a year or more above their students' present reading level. One teacher talked about her students crying, another was concerned about angry outbursts during testing, and another said it was not fair to frustrate and discourage kids.

Carol Hirschfeld, who taught reading at Harrington, has led a schoolwide emphasis on literature-based language arts teaching and a writing process approach; she is a continual resource and support for her teaching colleagues. When Carol was asked to be a language arts facilitator for the West Philadelphia Cluster, teachers were in tears at the thought of her leaving the school, which speaks to the dedication, care, and support that she gave to others during her long tenure at Harrington.

Some teachers have been involved in the Penn Literacy Network, as well as writing, math, and science workshops. Parents who are paraprofessionals are encouraged to attend the professional development workshops with the teachers, and a number of them do. Teachers have tried out a variety of professional development programs, and the principal does not impose or support one particular curriculum approach or philosophy. He says that the teachers can do whatever "works" (i.e., whatever moves their students ahead one grade level each year).

A lower-risk learning environment is created in many classrooms at Harrington. In one first-grade classroom this is done through a focus on group rather than individual behavior. The teacher encourages a "let's do this well together" attitude rather than a competitive me-against-you approach. Children are less likely to be singled out individually for either good or bad behavior, so there is less pressure to compete for individual attention.

In Christine Patterson's first-grade classroom, I observed a blackboard game wherein students went up to the board individually and erased the word that the teacher called out, from a list of words that were written there. When one child did not know the word she gave him, Christine said he could erase any word he knew. "It's okay not to know this one—just tell me what you *do* know"—a much lower-risk direction than having him guess and then calling the choice "wrong."

A Metaphor for Harrington: "This School Laughs"

"Some schools laugh and some don't. And this school laughs.
The first thing in the morning, you can hear the school laughing,
and I like that about a school."

Margaret Butler, program support teacher and previous teacher at the school for nineteen years, used the metaphor of the laughing school in an interview in her office. She clarifies the laughter as not just a "tee hee hee: I'm talking about a *hearty* laugh." When I asked what makes that happen, she talked about the "Harrington family" and how well they know each other:

> You walk into this place and someone always has something to say to someone, and there's laughter. It just starts. And if you listen, some of the comments may not be professional, but you know, in order for a person to make a comment to that person, they have to know them well enough. There has to be an understanding, there has to be a friendship in order for the person to verbalize something like that, and to elicit a *hearty* laugh.

Margaret also said, "You can pretty much sum up a school's personality the first ten minutes you're in the building, from the front door to the main office." When you walk into some schools in the morning, she added, "either you don't hear anything, or people pass in the halls going about their business. They don't mean to be rude, but you're just not there."

In Christine's room I heard some of this laughter. Her lighthearted reference to veteran teachers like herself was contained in the remark, "Some of us have been here *forever.*" And when she saw the unique book bag of a student whose father she had had in school, she said, "What is *that?* Only your father would think of something like that." Later, joking about student penmanship, she said, "If I can't read the letter, I'm not marking it correct. I'm not playing 'guess the letter.'"

In Margaret Bolden's room, a student was reprimanded for his sullen expression in a way that couldn't help but make him laugh. Margaret said, "If anyone's going to look angry, it's going to be *me.* I'm going to get on *your* nerves before you get on *mine.*" And at faculty meetings there was often a lighthearted tone. The faculty obviously enjoys sharing a good laugh.

Margaret Butler and I talked about the relationships and friendships at the school, including those with parents, and she added that trust was an important issue. When I asked how that trust was fostered, she said, "I think it comes from the fact that the majority of our faculty has been in place for so long, and they've learned to not only talk to, but talk *with* the parents."

The Arts Empower Program

Students at Harrington involved with the Arts Empower program have attended the Pennsylvania Ballet, the opera, and the symphony downtown in Philadelphia. The first year I observed at the school, students studied the story and the music from the ballet *Copellia* in class, and then took a field trip to see the performance downtown. After the performance, the students and their teachers talked with the choreographer about the ballet, and they learned about how much practice and revision goes into an event such as they had just seen. Teachers linked this important concept to the students' own writing and artwork, so they could better understand how much hard work goes into the production of any art form, whether it be dance, symphony, opera, drawing, painting, or writing.

The elegant examples of artwork produced by the students reflect the Arts Empower concepts of hard work, practice, and revision. Walking through the school is like walking through an art gallery. On one of my visits there was an African village displayed in the hallway as I entered the school. On another visit there was an Egyptian mummy along with a variety of other Egyptian artifacts created by the students on display outside Linda Kidd's classroom.

In the faculty lunchroom, during one of the wonderful monthly breakfast feasts organized by the teachers, I talked with art teacher Rosa Serota about the program and the school. I've included much of that interview here because it reveals an inspiring philosophy that is part of the culture of this school. Like Sarason's (1999) concept of teaching, Rosa describes student learning as a performing art.

Rosa (R): The arts are always performance based. They involve production, reflection, and revision. If they're the performing arts, they can be seen. In the art room when my kids do a piece of work, we finish the piece of work, all the work is put up, and it is discussed in terms of what we were supposed to learn. What did we see in the work? If it's a watercolor, do we see that somebody mastered how to use the watercolors? Do we see the patterns in the kente cloth?

Jill (J): And so there are criteria for every medium, then?

R: Yes, and there's also a discussion of A work, B work, C work, and D work. In my classroom, a piece of work has to be completed before you go to the next project, because you need to learn the skills in that piece to be able to use them in another piece.

Next week we have report card conferences and parents are going to come in. I am not going to show them the roll book with As, Bs, Cs, and Ds in it. I'm going to go get that child's folder. I'm going to show them the work and explain to them what in that work leads to that grade. The arts are always performance based. You can see what someone did.

J: What does that look like when they're going to the ballet, or when they're going to see an opera—what does that same sort of framework of thinking look like? What are you hoping for?

R: I'm hoping that they see production, revision, and reflection. I guess I can think of it best [as] when we saw the dress rehearsal of *The Nutcracker.* Leroy Keiser invited us to a dress rehearsal, and my kids went there at night, and they saw the process.

They saw Mr. Keiser have the dancers come out and, if any of the dancers weren't doing what he wanted them to do, he said, "Do it again. Do it again. Do it again." Until it was perfect. And when we came back to class and we talked about that, my kids said that really impressed them. They said, "It's like what we do—we have to do it until we get it right."

And I think what's really important about schools [is that] anything you do should be done in a way that's complete, and should be done not just the best you can do it to pass, the best you can do to get to the next level. But so that it's right. And if that feeling about school—completeness, doing the best, absolute best in one subject—is the criteria from kindergarten to fourth grade, then it's not hard to make it the criteria in every subject, whether the subject is literature or whether the subject is mathematics or science.

J: It seems to me the logical parallel there is with writing . . .

R: And that's why last year the Arts Empower teachers did their summer institute around writing.

J: And the motivation in all of this is to keep kids at that task—that hard, hard task of revising . . .

R: Of thinking like artists—that's the motivation. When an author writes, the author writes to have something published. That's a very high level of creativity. The author doesn't stop after three pages and say, "I don't think I can do any more." When an artist paints, an artist paints to finish something—to get a series. Maybe a painting that leads to another painting.

Scientists don't work with one experiment, and after they think they solve it, that's it. It becomes a way of thinking. And it begins to lead to other ways that you use that in your life. It begins to infiltrate the way you deal with everything.

PART II: EXPLORING THE THEMES

Relationships

As we saw in Chapter 2, the relationship themes common to the successful city schools I looked at include: valuing, appreciating, celebrating one another; care and support; empowerment; collaboration;

respect and trust across race and culture; democracy, personal choices, and individual freedom. What follows are some examples of these themes at Harrington.

A morning workshop in the science room, led by science teacher Jean Le Comte, illustrates the quality of the school-parent relationship. I sat with thirty-nine parents who were enjoying doughnuts and coffee as they made their own name tags, which set up the workshop as enjoyable from the start. Two mothers brought their young preschool children, and there were some fathers there too. Some of the paraprofessionals, who are also parents and grandparents, were there. Everyone had a good time and enjoyed the hands-on science experiments that were low cost and could easily be done at home. Supplies included toothpicks, string, cups, paper towels, popcorn, and Kleenex. The atmosphere was relaxed, social, and fun. There was laughter throughout the morning, parents joking and kidding with one another and with Jean, and much sharing of ideas.

In an after-school faculty meeting, the principal, Larry Colvin, said (in anticipation of his retirement and replacement) that he didn't want the chemistry of the school to change. But he also said that the teachers were so good that "I don't think anyone can get in the way."

After a meeting with teachers from other schools in the West Philadelphia Cluster, Loretta Pugh, Randi Gaier, Rosa Serota, and Gayle Martin commented in their own faculty meeting about the choices, freedom, and democratic relationships that they have at Harrington:

Loretta: We have a good school—nobody tells us what to do. We need to find out who is coming in here and not mess up what we have—keep the decision making and school-based management going.

Randi: We all have ideas about what we are doing—we're not ordered or moved around.

Gayle: We are really lucky here—others have no choice in learning communities. We have flexibility.

Rosa: Others don't know what a learning community is [whereas they have worked together collaboratively in their Arts Empower community for several years].

Community assistants tell me that they feel respected and that their children love the teachers, who care about them in return. In a meeting in the library they talk about their valuable role in the school, the way they work together with the teachers, helping special-needs kids as well as others. They feel that they are empowered to help make decisions, and that the teachers really care and have the children's interests at heart.

At 10 A.M. in the faculty lunchroom, after another bountiful faculty breakfast, I listen as classroom assistants talk about the open relationships in the school. They tell me that they can voice their opinions and that they have the freedom to do their own work the way they want. They say that nobody turns their nose up at them—instead, they are made to feel comfortable. And no one checks up on them or accuses them of not working hard enough when they might be resting their head or feeling unwell. "If you have a dispute, you say what you have to say and it's over—you go on from there." At other schools, they say, everybody walks around with frowns on their faces.

Teachers show respect and care for children and families in and out of their classrooms. Debbie Williams is respectful of the culture and language of her students and their families, incorporating their language into her lessons. She suggests that white teachers invite their African American students to teach them about street language, dialects, and slang. She believes that it is important to use words and phrases that her students are familiar with. Discussing the definition of *advice* during her reading lesson, she used examples such as, "You're giving them 'the news.'" Or, "You're telling them what's 'ready to go down.'"

Care and support of low-progress students is evident in Kate Walsh's second-grade class. One child, Jay, looked to me like an average student as I observed in early April. Kate gave Jay many opportunities to participate, both orally and in writing on the board, which he did with only one error (misspelling *blue*). He contributed an example of a modern-day fable, read orally with only one miscue (*did not* for *didn't*), and only became nonparticipatory when he was frustrated by his own perfectionism. This last problem was solved when Kate noticed his head down and gave him a new piece of paper.

Kate is attentive to Jay's needs, celebrates his strengths and contributions, and makes him feel a part of the classroom family—so much so that I couldn't have picked him out as a problem learner. I was surprised when Kate later told me that Jay is a low-progress student.

Orchestration of Learning

As described in Chapter 2, the orchestration of learning themes include: meaningful, growthful curriculum that is social, personal, integrative, transforming, and ecological; congruent/authentic evaluation; adequate human and material resources; time for reflection; and administration that is supportive.

In the classrooms where I observed (all of the first- and second-grade classrooms and one third-grade classroom) students were actively engaged in reading real books, talking thoughtfully and inquiringly about books and authors, writing creatively and expressively about their own ideas and questions, about their own lives, and about what they were learning in social studies, art, math, and science.

Low-progress students like Jay could do well in these activities because they are activities that require more than one right answer. They encourage students to take risks, to make the mistakes that are vital to meaningful learning, and to be creative. Where Jay and others like him, who are not precisely "on schedule" with their peers, have problems is in the competitive and decontextualized performances and tests that are not connected to authentic, meaningful learning. In standardized and fragmented testing situations, both teachers and students say they are frustrated, depressed, angry, and demoralized. Their knowledge and expertise is not honored and valued, and precious time in the classroom is used up with preparing for, taking, and recovering from commercial textbook publishers' tests.

Loretta Pugh's after-school club gives students a choice between reading and computers. The two computer groups of five students each have a student leader, and the groups work together well, with each member given a fair amount of time to explore, collaborate, and socialize. The reading group is led at first by Loretta, who shares *Corn Is Maize,* a book about the many uses of corn. They chat together about ideas in the book. Several students then read the books they brought to their group of six students.

In Marie Marvil's first-grade classroom, students are enthusiastically acting out *Hello House,* a Brer Rabbit story, using only a brown sheet of paper as a house and six very simply made brown paper masks for the wolf, Brer Rabbit, and others. Several casts of players perform the story with dialogue and expression after Marie has read it with them chorally, rehearsed and coached the rabbit and wolf parts expressively, heard several retellings, and talked about the meaning of the story. Following the dramatizations, the students write in their journal about a favorite part of the story.

Christine's classroom assistant (a parent) uses a meaning-focused approach to working with her small group of readers. Christine says that Starla has helped bring these low-progress readers up to an average level by working with them for much of the day, giving them the special attention they need. Starla gives meaning hints, and she has students reread when the narrative does not make sense to them. She will give them words as needed to keep the meaning flowing, not diverting to skill drills.

Christine's empowerment/transformation teaching includes a book on the Underground Railroad. She tells her first graders that the slaves would have done *anything* in the world to learn to read and write, then asks why slave owners were afraid of letting slaves read and write. Jamar says, "They didn't want them to be smart."

Linda Kidd's empowerment teaching affects the whole school in her role as social studies support teacher. She believes that students should know their culture, because you can only take pride in your race if you celebrate it. Together with Debbie Williams, she created a schoolwide thematic approach to Native American culture, taught from September to December; African American culture was covered from January to June. A parent workshop on making African instruments was very successful, and a schoolwide celebration evolved. Debbie and Linda made a decision to go beyond the eight Arts Empower classrooms, to expose classes schoolwide to this curriculum, thereby empowering all students and their families.

In Debbie William's third-grade classroom, the morning begins with students going about the business of getting organized for learning while listening to music. Debbie tells her students that they are the smartest kids in the school, and she fills them with hopes, dreams, and belief in their own possibilities. She teaches them to think about the process of learning: "Know how you got the answer." And she asks them, "What were you thinking about? Why are you doing that?"

She motivates them to read for meaning and to read with expression: "Make me want to know about *Jumanji!*" she tells them as they read the story. Her vocabulary words include *respect, wisdom,* and *astonished;* she illustrates with Ebonics ("You go girl!") when defining what their mother might say when astonished.

Her partnership relationship with parents includes calling them two weeks before school begins and asking for a family representative to come meet with her the first day of school. She tells them she needs them there, and she explains her rules and what she needs from them. She gets 100 percent participation.

Monthly field trips in Randi Gaier's first-grade classroom include destinations such as the zoo, an orchard, a plantation, a firehouse, a farm, an art museum, and a Puerto Rican museum. These enrichment outings occur in other classrooms as well.

What Do the Students Say?

The students themselves can tell us much about the quality of the learning process. Randi Gaier's students see themselves as good readers because, as they say, "we read every day and every night."

Christine Patterson's first graders talk with her about how the teacher helped them to read:

> You read to us and we read
>
> When the teacher reads, you follow with your finger
>
> We read signs
>
> We have fun tests

The students also talk about how people at home help them to read:

> We read to them
>
> They read bedtime stories
>
> They let you read it by yourself
>
> They help with words, and help so you can do it by yourself

And Christine's students talk about the many places they like to read:

> In my closet
>
> In my bed with a night-light
>
> In my mom's room
>
> On the bus
>
> With food
>
> In a quiet place

The Environment

The theme of environment or climate for teaching and learning includes: opportunities for risk taking, making mistakes, experimenting; commitment and motivation for change and growth; ownership and empowerment; working hard and being hopeful activists; a comfortable family of caring community members who trust and respect each other; a fun place where people laugh and enjoy one another.

The joyful atmosphere—laughing, learning, and sharing—at the parent workshop on science reflected the tone of the school. The coffee, tea, and doughnuts, as well as the presence of young children, made it seem like a family occasion. People were obviously comfortable with one another, and enjoyed being at the school in this science classroom with a teacher who some of them had in elementary school. The issue of committed teachers who remain at the school for a long time and continue to motivate and encourage the parents and families is important as well. Many of the teachers are teaching the children of their former students, which creates an "extended family" school.

The Arts Empower program includes after-school parent and student workshops in the art room, surrounding participants with a rich variety of artwork, prints, and inspiring models of creative work done by students. The classroom field trips to the ballet, to plays, and to other cultural events include parents along with the teachers and students, and provide a motivating environment as well as a low-risk family atmosphere for learning about and enjoying the arts.

Language arts are included in the after-school workshop on writing, and one paraprofessional continued thinking about and experimenting with a word she had been introduced to, long after the workshop was over. She was working on pronouncing *ubiquitous* for the next several days when I talked with her in the hallway, suggesting an environment of risk taking, experimenting, and motivation to grow and learn.

On the issue of empowerment, the staff has decided to be involved in the selection of the new principal, since they feel that they have the right to be a part of the process. During their teachers union meeting they talked about how much control they thought they could have over the selection, and they elected a representative to be on the selection committee along with a community member, a parent, and the cluster leader, Dr. Butler.

Despite some discouragement from the Pennsylvania Federation of Teachers (PFT) union representative and the negative experiences of other schools, Harrington teachers decided to be open to possibilities, to be hopeful, and to keep working at being a part of the democratic process because they felt that (1) they had earned the right to be a part of the selection process by being one of the first schools to do school-based management and self-governance, (2) their involvement would show they care, and (3) they should have a voice in their school's leadership. They decided to write up a job description including their own criteria for a new principal.

A family atmosphere is created at Harrington at the monthly breakfasts: the faculty lunchroom looks like a bountiful family dining room table. Every seat around the room-length table is taken and there are many people standing. The table is filled with large trays of various kinds of bagels with assorted cream cheese spreads, trays of assorted doughnuts, a variety of coffee cakes, casseroles and brunch dishes, and fresh fruit. A beautiful plant serves as a centerpiece. A coffee carafe and orange juice are on a table in a corner of the room.

The family group includes teachers, classroom assistants, and other staff members who socialize, laugh, share stories, and enjoy one another's company. This feast was prepared by a group of teachers. Next month a group of parents and classroom assistants will organize the once-a-month breakfast feast. People come and go throughout the morning, and the feast continues from 8 A.M. until after 10 A.M., when some assistants and teachers begin to put things together so they can be eaten at lunchtime. At 11:30 there were still a few plates, trays, and boxes of food for the staff to nibble on with their lunches.

Christine's after-school reading club also looks like a family gathering, as the first- though fourth-grade children sit on the rug for an hour, listening to books being read. An older student reads for a while as another student checks children in at a desk. Tony, the tearful little boy who I met at Loretta's club, is free to wander around the room and watch the fish in the tank (a girl tells me that this is Tony's favorite thing to do). Christine shares some of her favorite books. One is a book with colorful pictures of exotic Amazon animals, which elicits many interested comments and questions.

The Process of Change: It Takes a Whole Village

Change and growth at Harrington are supported by the powerful combination of:

1. individual dedication to the pursuit of important and relevant knowledge (such as through development of the Native American and African thematic studies and the Arts Empower program)
2. collaborating with and supporting fellow colleagues

3. learning and coordinating with small learning communities (SLCs)

4. a commitment to making knowledge available to all students, parents, and teachers in the school (the concept of school as a family/village)

5. financial support from foundations, grants, and the school district

6. including parents as paraprofessionals and respected colleagues in the school, asking what workshops they want, and making them feel welcome

One example, described more fully in Chapter 1, illustrates this combination. Because Harrington is 98 percent African American, Debbie Williams saw the need to develop a thematic study of African culture, history, and geography not only for her third-grade classroom but for the whole school. Having gathered some resources and given some thought to this project, she approached Linda Kidd to collaborate with her on developing the study. In addition to their combined knowledge as elementary teachers, Linda's areas of expertise included literature and role-play, and Debbie's included music. Furthermore, the Arts Empower SLC added African printmaking and other African art knowledge to the mix.

The result of this fertile combination of interest, talent, and collaborative pursuit was an extended thematic study of several African countries along with African American studies that continued for half of the year. Individual classroom teachers chose particular countries and particular works of literature that fit best with the interests of the students as well as the curriculum for that grade and class. Extended schoolwide involvement was possible through the social studies teacher, who saw all grade levels. A student project involving the construction of African instruments extended to a parent workshop, which drew a large number of families into the school.

Working together as a whole school in an area of study of significance to the students and their families was an important goal of this project. This is a good example of the way the Harrington family works together in a collaborative and enriching way for the benefit of the students. Just as SLCs work together, the larger school family functions as a supportive and collaborative unit. The goal of including parents and families in the work of the school is an important part of this. Particularly in the case of family culture and history, including parents in the projects of the children broadens the notion of "school as family" to "community as extended family."

REFLECTION: WHAT STOOD OUT FOR ME

☐ A committed and collaborative staff remains willing to try new things and plan together for the successful learning of students.

☐ Inviting parents as well as paraprofessionals as family workshop participants in the school helps create an "extended family" community.

☐ A warm family environment enables laughter and fun along with learning.

☐ Celebration of the language and culture of the children and their families instills pride and self-worth in students.

☐ Including the arts—ballet, symphony, opera—in the curriculum enriches the learning experience of all.

5

Barriers, Failures, and Problematic Solutions

Are there students who are failing in the Taylor and Harrington Elementary Schools? Are there teachers who resist student-centered alternatives to literacy teaching and testing? Are there teacher-student relationships and teacher-parent relationships that are not working well? Are there, in fact, all of the same problems that other schools in and out of the city have as they strive to meet the needs of all students? Yes indeed.

Using the case study of one low-progress learner, we will look more closely at some of the barriers to successful city learning, within the context of developing the full potential of all learners. We make the radical assumption here that all students have potential. So it is the job of the teacher, in collaboration with the school curriculum support staff, the district office staff, parents, the state and federal education department advisers, and the leadership of our state and federal government to ensure that each student has a wide variety of personally meaningful opportunities to learn, supported by adequate resources and services.

I followed several high- and low-progress learners in each elementary classroom to better understand the complex ecology of city children. My focus was on learning to read and write, since my background and area of interest is language arts. In Teresa Alvarez's second-grade classroom I observed Ciara, a low-progress student. She is one of the smallest children in the class, and she has not progressed much over the year, as compared with Domingo, who has done very well.

As I observed Ciara's meaning making during a phonics activity, I saw that she was actually attempting to "make sense" of an abstract exercise on hard and soft *c* sounds. When Teresa asked whether the letter *c* in the word *pencil* has a hard or soft sound, Ciara immediately said, "hard," though the *c* sound in *pencil* is soft. And for the word *cake* that followed, she said "soft," though the correct answer is hard. When I asked Ciara about her answer for the *cake* item, she explained her reasoning by saying that cake is soft (i.e., it feels soft when you touch it), which is a sensible reply for a seven-year-old.

The workbook exercise required students to color the picture if the word has a hard sound, and circle the picture if the sound is soft, using word examples such as *face, cap, clock, cup, mice, dice, pencil,* and *cake.* The exercise—focusing on the abstract letter sounds, the one sounding like a *k* (hard) and the other sounding like an *s* (soft), and remembering to choose between circling and coloring one or the other, all while ignoring the context of the meaning of the given words (e.g., what *cake* actually signified)—seemed inherently confusing even to me, and I have my doctorate in language arts and family literacy.

Ciara made the reasonable decision to make contextual sense of this activity, but her answers were not "correct" according to the textbook company. Similar items will be found on the standardized tests that Ciara will be required to take, and her inherent sense-making will be similarly discredited. Teachers in classrooms where portfolios and work sampling include observations of students engaged in authentic, unstandardized reading and writing activities have a better chance of seeing Ciara's potential. But the mandated bottom line for all U.S. schools is still the standardized test score.

Problematic Solution #1: Textbook Literacy Content

So what is the problem here? Is it the decontextualized nature of the phonics exercise, which goes against Ciara's instinct that the activity should make sense? Is it the abstract nature of the task—circle/color the item with a hard/soft sound—that is not appropriate, considering a seven-year-old beginning reader's way of reading the world and the word? Is it the use of fragmented, disconnected activities that teach children that reading is senseless and difficult, rather than natural and meaning filled? Is it the poverty of the definition of *reading* that drives the production of these textbook and workbook exercises, as well as the tests that match them?

Research on the reading processes informs us that it is all of the above—and more. Richard Allington (1995, 1998) adds to this the disproportionate amount of time that "poor readers" are subjected to such meaningless and abstract tasks, while the "good readers" get to actually spend their time reading real books. And he provides multiple examples of the way that the rich get richer and the poor (readers) get poorer in this inequitable process.

Gerald Coles (2000) adds the important issue of the content of the literacy activities, and the social class differences and lack of opportunity that constrain literacy learning for children in poverty. Describing the powerful impact of poverty on learning to read, Coles writes:

> It is not surprising that the one hundred worst performing schools . . . were clustered in the poorest neighborhoods. The harsh conditions of poverty—such as excessive work, excessive hours, insufficient income, no medical insurance, and substandard housing—hinder low-income parents from devoting adequate time and energy to their children's literacy experience and from being able to allocate funds for literacy materials. (97)

Middle-class or affluent families can provide more opportunities and advantages, which has a different impact on student learning. Coles cites one school official as saying, "We were always very successful academically when our kids were coming from middle-class families" (97).

Middle-Class Opportunities and Advantages

The advantages come in several forms. Frank Smith (1986) tells us that this includes enlarged bases of experience and vocabulary, a multitude of story frames from which to make sense of new stories, and many personal experiences (in collaboration with more literate coaches) with printmaking, story sharing, oral and written composing, and language play. Opportunities for social interaction with other children of similar ages are also an important part of this, since learning is social as well as experiential and personal. Smith describes the benefits of social learning as joining the "literacy club."

Many middle- and upper-middle-class children have additional experience with well-resourced, experience-based literature, art- and music-filled preschool programs like the Montessori Schools, Waldorf Schools, preschools using an Emilio Reggio model, well-designed community nursery schools, and other private preschool programs. This may be in addition to exposure to art, music, dance, theater, and sports lessons and activities; or family trips and vacations that include visits to museums and historical places; and other opportunities to build a wealth of experiences and knowledge for making sense of the world of print.

Children who have had many preschool experiences with print, who have had many stories read to them, who have had the leisure, resources, and encouragement to play with written language in their homes have a distinct advantage. So do those who have had many opportunities to have a more experienced reader and writer mentor them in their highly literate homes. They have discovered the world of print in a natural, socially and economically secure, personally interesting and child-centered way.

This is not to say that poor families do not have literacy-rich homes and culturally and linguistically rich oral and written language traditions, for Taylor and Dorsey-Gaines (1988), Heath (1983), Cummins (1989), Moll (1992), and many other ethnographic researchers have documented quite the opposite. But it is to say that freedom from poverty, joblessness, and homelessness allows families to experience better nutrition and health, more opportunities for the time to read and write with children, more reading and writing materials in the home, and more security and hopefulness about learning and literacy and life.

The security of not having to worry about enough nutritious food for your children to eat, or whether the heat or electricity will be turned off, or whether there will be angry arguments at home, gunshots at night, alcohol- or drug-related problems, or other family crises makes it infinitely easier to concentrate on language learning. Since reading is meaning making, and since, as Paulo Freire reminds us, reading the world comes before reading the word, it helps if one's world is sensible, relatively stable, safe, and hopeful.

Ciara's World

Preschools with enriched opportunities to learn are virtually nonexistent in poor neighborhoods like Ciara's. Head Start, the only public preschool program available for low-income children, can only serve 10 percent of the eligible children in poor urban communities (Kozol 2000). Ciara lives in a high-poverty, crime- and drug-infested urban community where gunshots are heard nearly every night. The city trash removal is unpredictable in her neighborhood, and the response from law enforcement authorities can be less than immediate.

Because of the crime and danger in the neighborhood, Ciara's mother tells me, children stay inside. They can't go outside to meet and play with friends, so much of the social learning and "literacy club" benefits accessible to middle-class children are not available to Ciara. Families may not even know many of their neighbors on the block, because people stay in their houses, are fearful of the danger in the community, and may be fearful and distrustful of new people moving in.

Near Ciara's school it took the death of a five-year-old and her grandfather, along with a subsequent citizen's march on city hall, to get a traffic light to slow down the traffic—traffic that continues to boom and roar loudly outside her classroom windows every day. Beside her school playground, a trash- and junk-littered lot contains old tires, broken glass, and needles that the children see every day.

A group of parents, members of EPOP, have organized and written many letters and marched to the slumlord's office to see him several times. I was impressed by their fierce determination and hopeful persistence when I marched with them in October after one of their organizing meetings at the school. They wrote and tried to visit to plead for their children's safety and clean surroundings, all of which he has ignored. They also reported his community neglect (which includes abandoned crack houses) to the Licensing and Inspection office over the past year, but nothing has been done. Five years later the trash, litter, and graffitied crack houses remain for the children to walk by every day.

When I ask Ciara to tell me about herself as a reader, to try to get a sense of her literacy-learning history and her strategies for learning to read, she wants to tell me instead about difficulties at home—the family crises that they are experiencing. Her mother recently sent a note to Teresa asking for any leftover milk from their classroom breakfasts, because she is short of milk for their new baby. Ciara's father had difficulty in school, like so many other Latino students, and he assumes that both he and Ciara have a learning disability. His dependency on alcohol to cope with feelings of incompetence and joblessness has resulted in many angry encounters at home.

This is Ciara's world. A less than safe, sense-filled, hopeful place to live and learn and grow. What does an urban elementary school do to help students like Ciara? How do they begin to provide the sense-making experiences that she needs, and that her community, city, and society have not developed or supported sufficiently? How do they respond to her family? How do they attempt to prevent her from becoming another statistic, when as reported by ASPIRA the Latino failure and dropout rate in Philadelphia and New York City—a rate that has been consistent for the past two decades—is 80 percent?

Taylor's Response to Ciara

Teresa keeps her students for two years (a process called "looping"), because spending two years with a child gives the teacher the opportunity to know the child and family better and to build a trusting relationship with them. The teacher can extend to them the concern and respect evident in Teresa's response to Ciara's mother, sending milk home and coaching Ciara to read when things are difficult at home. Another example of Taylor's care and support is the after-school dance club Ciara loves, led by Debby Perry.

Ciara plays school at home because she loves her school and wants to become a teacher, which shows the positive influence that Taylor has had on her. The family environment in the classroom where Ciara can have social time to be with friends, and have "breakfast with our friends" is yet another way she is supported and cared for in school. These opportunities for social learning are vital for literacy club membership, especially in urban communities where fear causes more isolation from other people.

What Taylor cannot do is provide for Ciara what the city and society do not provide: equal access to meaningful and useful education for her parents so they can have equal access to employment and decent housing; equal opportunities to experience a safe and experientially rich community environment where she can live, and grow, and learn; an economic safety net so that no child goes hungry; and an opportunity to develop hopefulness about her own possibilities in the future and the future of her family.

I am reminded of the traditional advice to fathers, which could as well be offered to policymakers: the best way to show that you care about your children is to care for their mother. The majority of those who live in poverty in the United States are children, and the next highest group is their mothers. We cannot impoverish one out of every two African American and Latino mothers and children, and then expect them to do well in school. Their poverty ensures instead their continued school failure rates.

Successful learning is social, personal, integrative, transformative, and embedded within the larger ecology of the learner. It is interconnected and interdependent with the family, the school, the community, and the larger society. And it is dependent upon the health, education, and welfare of the whole family. To take a narrow, skill-focused approached to teaching and evaluating the learning of students like Ciara, removed from the ecology that shapes and constrains their learning, is the height of illiterate and reductionistic thinking. Yet that is exactly the "solution" that politicians and policymakers continue to advocate and mandate.

Problematic Solution #2: Standardized Testing

It was not possible for me to talk with Ciara while she was taking a standardized district or state test, but in her children's book, *First Grade Takes a Test,* Miriam Cohen (1980) gives us a wonderful child's-eye view of standardized-test taking. In the book, a first grader named George is looking at the test, which reads:

Rabbits eat
(1) lettuce (2) dog food (3) sandwiches

George raises his hand and tells his teacher, "Rabbits have to eat carrots, or their teeth will get too long and stick into them." The teacher nods and smiles, but puts her finger to her lips to quiet George. George then carefully draws a picture of a carrot on the test so the test people will learn what rabbits need.

Another test item in Cohen's story is:

What do firemen do?
(1) make bread (2) put out fires (3) sing

Sammy reads this and pokes Willy, saying, "Firemen get your head out when it's stuck. My uncle had his head stuck in a big pipe, and the firemen came and got it out." But none of the choices offered this, so Sammy got that item wrong on the test. But Sammy could write a richly creative story about what firemen do, if he were given the chance.

Children are inherent sense-makers, as we have learned from over half a century of research on learning to read by Holdaway (1979), Goodman and Goodman (1989), Clay (1997), Smith (1986), Halliday (1978), Vygotsky (1978), and Freire (1981). Ciara is certainly making sense when she says that cake is soft. Yet we disregard all of the research and common sense, opting instead for what Coles (2000) calls "The bad science that hurts children." And so, content-poor workbook exercises and the ecologically invalid use of standardized test scores to evaluate reading will continue to negatively impact upon Ciara, her teachers, and her school.

In addition, the continued use of standardized tests will drive the school and classroom curriculum in the direction of teaching to the tests, particularly in schools within poor neighborhoods like Ciara's, and particularly in schools with high proportions of children of color, wherein test scores are generally low for all of the social and economic reasons that we have discussed above. Similarly, students like Ciara will be given more abstract, confusing, decontextualized (and therefore less meaningful and sensible) exercises and fewer opportunities to share what they really know and can learn. For example, in nearby Harrisburg, Pennsylvania, the superintendent announced that the district will teach to the tests because they have no choice. They are under threat of school takeover for low test scores.

What Is the Alternative?

One hundred years ago, the insightful education philosopher John Dewey told us that learning demands active engagement in personally meaningful experiences. Dewey (1916) saw education at its best as an exercise in democracy, preparing the student to be an actively engaged citizen.

Eighty years ago another great educator, Lev Vygotsky, described tests as fossilized views of yesterday's learning. Any test, he said, can only measure learning that is in the past. By contrast, real learning potential can only be measured in what Vygotsky (1978) called the zone of proximal development. Within this zone of potential, the learner is working collaboratively with a more capable peer or mentor who continually leads the learner ahead to more complex thinking and learning.

So the alternative to measuring dead or fossilized learning outside of sensible contexts is to evaluate learning that is alive and sensible; learning that is personally meaningful, learning in which the student is actively engaged in a collaborative pursuit of knowledge, learning that leads the student ahead into increasingly complex thinking. We have a wide variety of alternative evaluation methods that are active, socially constructed, and personally engaging. They are also meaningful learning activities, so that teaching, learning, and evaluation are interconnected. A few examples of evaluation methods that are rich in meaning and value include:

- writing for real-world purposes (Sammy could actually write about firemen and tell his story)
- student portfolios of work, developed over time, in collaboration with teachers and parents

- projects that are school- or community-based, developed in collaboration with community members, teachers, and peers
- exhibits of personally researched and thoughtfully developed student work, such as history projects
- dialogue journals exchanged among students, teachers, and parents
- reading/literature response logs that encourage student choice and voice
- science and math logs that document the thinking and learning process as well as the correct answers
- student and teacher conferences, including parents in some of these to embrace the richness and diversity of family literacy and learning
- running records of reading, and tape recordings of oral reading taken at several points during the year
- checklists and anecdotal records kept by both students and teachers
- oral discussions and debates
- science experiments and projects developed by the student in collaboration with teachers and peers
- math problems, questions, and projects developed by students that are personally meaningful and useful

In the publications of national and international education associations such as NCTE, NAEYC, NCSS, NSTA, NCTM, AERA, IRA, NCREST, Kappa Delta Pi, Phi Delta Kappa, and many others, there are abundant examples and rich descriptions of valid forms of evaluation: evaluations that put value in learners and their authentic learning; evaluations that measure the actual learning of students in the contexts that give them meaning.

Likewise, many publishers, such as Heinemann, Teachers College, Jossey-Bass, Christopher Gordon, Stenhouse, and Richard C. Owen publish excellent teacher-written books that provide meaningful and valid alternatives to standardized teaching and testing.

Authors such as Linda Darling-Hammond, Ancess, and Falk (1995), Ann Lieberman and Lynn Miller (1999), Peter Johnston (1992), Pat Carini (1979), Lois Bridges (1995), and Jane Hansen (1998) have studied and described meaningful evaluation from the individual to the classroom and school levels. We have international models from England, such as *The Primary Language Record* (Barrs et al. 1989), and from Australia and New Zealand (see curriculum documents from the Ministries of Education.)

We do not lack the research and the models. We lack the collective will to courageously confront an increasingly inequitable and disfranchising system of schooling, and to combine our best professional knowledge and research in the service of the educational human rights of all of our children.

John Goodlad (1987) reported rampant boredom in U.S. schools in the 1980s as a result of mind-numbing textbooks and a test-driven standardization of teaching. In the 1990s schools reported more alienation and increased frustration and violence. The challenge for both teacher education and student learning in the twenty-first century is to go beyond what Goodlad (2000) calls a "myopic concentration" on "high-stakes tests spawned by the accountability movement which has pushed aside the profound issues of schooling we should be addressing" (89).

Goodlad goes on to describe the kind of education that develops individuals "in the context of justice, fairness, responsibility, and mutual caring to which the Declaration of Independence and the Constitution [and I would add the Universal Declaration of Human Rights] speak so eloquently":

> The challenge is to spell out and implement the role of education . . . in developing civil, civic, and ecological democratic character. . . . The school mission of educating the youth for satisfying, responsible participation in a social and political democracy is endangered if that society is democratic in name but not in understanding and functioning. (88–89)

The city teaching that I have observed, when it was developed in a democratic environment of collaboration and mutual respect, has the power to transform teaching and learning in the way that Goodlad describes. The possibility for a more enlightened and growthful way of teaching and evaluating student learning lies before us. We have only to support its rebirth and commit ourselves to collective change.

REFLECTION: WHAT STOOD OUT FOR ME

☐ Problematic "solutions" are perhaps our greatest barriers to successful reading and learning.

☐ The poverty of the textbook curriculum and the fragmentation and meaninglessness of standardized testing create failure for the children who are in most need of meaningful reading.

☐ Even caring, supportive, and knowledgeable teachers and schools cannot ensure successful learning for all students without equally supportive and knowledgeable social and economic policies—without just and fair health and welfare supports for all children and families.

☐ Continuous, meaningful evaluation methods that are rooted in observation and in the context of authentic learning experiences can help to ensure the success of all students.

6

Preparing City Teachers
Linking with the Community

IN COLLABORATION WITH WANDA DAVIS, EDWARD BAILEY,
AND SHELLI PALMER FELTON

*You need to have a desire and a hunger to want to see people
learn. And if you don't, and it's just a job, then you ought to
change and do something else. But you shouldn't talk about
teaching, because you have to have a love of people. And if you
have a love of people—kids learn.*

—REV. EDWARD BAILEY, 1997

In 1991 Mrs. Wanda Davis noticed during a church play practice that
the children were having difficulty reading their parts. She realized that
the schools were not doing enough to help their children learn to read,
and she decided to begin a tutoring program. For a year she appealed
to the church leadership and to a university professor she'd been referred to, but she found no support. Then in 1993 Rev. Edward Bailey
came to the church, and she found the backing to begin the program.

The Bethel African Methodist Episcopal Church community in
Lancaster, Pennsylvania, is committed to their children and to the
Lancaster community, so they took on this responsibility to help children after school with reading and math. They bought back from the
school district an older school building behind the church, which was
originally a Freedom School, and turned it into a cultural center for
the community. The center provided a space for tutoring, for a computer room, and for a variety of programs for children and adults.

When I look back over my experiences with Wanda and with the
tutoring program over the past few years, one memory stands out. It is
of an evening that I spent with her, one of many when I stayed over-
night with her in Lancaster after tutoring rather than drive the sixty-
five miles to my home in Carlisle. Usually I stayed over on Thursday

99

nights after the 5–6:30 P.M. tutoring session, and we would go to choir practice from 7 to 9 P.M. before going home. I loved those evenings, because the music would stay with me throughout the following week, the lyrics floating out at unexpected times, or I'd find myself humming lines of music that we had practiced, such as "I want mercy that suits my case—personalized . . . individualized . . ." or, "Bring the ones who are weary, bring them all to the water . . ." or, "Bring the children without might, easy the load and light."

This was a Monday evening, however, and after the children went home at 6:30 P.M. and we cleaned up after snack time (Mrs. Davis' "snacks" range from trays of peanut butter and jelly crackers to pots of her delicious soups), we went to her home to make soup for the family of Raheem, an eleven-year-old boy who had come regularly for tutoring. We were greeted warmly with hugs by Raheem's father who said, despite the terrible emotional pain that he was feeling, how well Raheem had been doing in school since he was in the tutoring program.

"He got Student of the Month, and he was on the honor roll!" his father said with much emotion. And he proudly told us how responsible Raheem had become, getting up to fix his own breakfast and even ironing his own shirt sometimes in the morning.

Raheem's mother was in bed, he told us, and she has had great difficulty in getting up or in talking with people for the past two days. But he went to get her so that Mrs. Davis could talk with her for a moment. When Raheem's mother came down, she thanked Mrs. Davis through tear-filled eyes, and accepted her gifts of soup, and love, and deepest sympathy. As I too hugged Raheem's parents, I was overcome with the emotion that filled the room.

The previous week Raheem was one of the many energetic students attending the tutoring program at Bethel AME, where our college students come to work along with parents and community members. In one of my student's journals, Raheem was described as one of the bright and interested students that she so enjoyed being with. Then on Friday he came home with a mysterious illness—he had a headache and was feeling sick. When he continued feeling sick and his fever shot up alarmingly on Saturday morning, his parents rushed him to the local hospital. And on Saturday afternoon he died—of spinal meningitis.

His father found out later that parents at some of the schools had gotten a warning that there were a few reported cases of meningitis, and that other students had been treated successfully. Raheem's family, however, did not get this information. Raheem's father wasn't blaming anyone for this. He just wished that he would have known.

After we left Raheem's home we went to take soup to a neighbor who had lost a leg and was confined to a wheelchair. She and Wanda had been friends for many years, and we stayed for a while to visit. Then we went to Sandy Cornish's home to take soup to her, since she had not been feeling well lately. Sandy helps Wanda every Monday and Thursday with the tutoring program, even though she works daily until 5 P.M., as Wanda does, and sometimes works evenings. This evening she was at work, so we left the soup with her husband.

Beginning Our Partnership

Our college-community partnership with Bethel AME began with an evening seminar at Elizabethtown College. After spending the 1996–1997 year in Philadelphia and New York City, I returned to teaching with a renewed commitment to social justice, interracial understanding, and preparing teachers for the rich diversity of students who will be in their future classrooms. I gathered together some of my friends, and invited them to join me in beginning a serious dialogue about race and teacher preparation on campus.

Reverend Bailey visited my fall 1997 Diversity and Urban Education seminar, along with Tracy Jackson, president of Colors United, an interracial student group committed to celebrating diversity; Phindile Shongwe, a communications student from Swaziland; and Shelli Palmer, then a preservice social studies teacher (and presently my son Patrick's excellent high school teacher). We talked together informally about some of the issues and problems that prevent deeper interracial understanding and communication.

During that three-hour evening class, Shelli Palmer shared her past experiences as an African American student in a "good" suburban high school. Shelli was part of a ten-year qualitative case study of an African American student whose learning was denied in his majority white school (Bartoli 1995), and an oral history project in our hometown (Palmer et al. 1991). She described some of the problems that exist in teacher-preparation programs:

> The classes where we have the open discussions about racial and ethnic differences, and ways to go about making sure our classrooms are diverse places to foster children's development, are electives. And in the classes that we have to take, we don't talk about what we need to talk about to succeed in our classrooms.

And we don't really have any exposure with any kind of diverse students. If you do, it's initiated on your own. You travel yourself to schools to get the exposure you need to be a good teacher. It's really sad, because until we fix these problems in the teacher-training process, the things that happen to people like "James" and myself are just going to continue to happen. What are we doing to combat the problem? And that's what the real issue is: What are we doing to change it?

Phindile Shongwe shared her experiences as an African student in a white college and her discouragement with the lack of multicultural understanding and knowledge at the college level. For example, one professor argued with her about whether or not there was snow in Africa, and people have asked, "Do you have a phone in Africa?" and "Do you have ice cream?"

I am from Swaziland in southern Africa. I grew up in South Africa, so I still have homes in both South Africa and Swaziland. You get a professor talking about Africa as one great big country, and they do not want to distinguish the different countries. There are so many different things happening there. We are definitely one people; but the way we live, and the things we do, and the economy *is* just so different. Someone said to me, "Oh you're from Africa. Do you know so and so from Ghana?"

Phindi saw the problem as people not taking an interest in reading and learning about other people, and being satisfied with a very limited realm of existence:

They talk about going out and meeting other people, but they don't take the time, and they don't show the interest to start reading about other people before they go there. For people who want to be teachers. . . . I'd say it would be better for you to start learning about the children you are going to be teaching, the communities you are going to be teaching in—read about them and ask questions. Because that's another thing—students here do not ask questions.

Tracy Jackson described her experience as a former education major. She shared her dismay with textbooks that preached diversity yet treated African American, Latino, and Asian students as "different" and in need of being taught in a special (and often stereotypical) way:

And [we say] this is how we have to teach them because they're different. And we make that difference seem like this is going to be more work for you. And more work, we tend to think, is a negative. That really struck me, and it worried me about the future of education. Coming up in the system myself, I felt cheated. I learned a lot about Washington and Lincoln, but what happened to Frederick Douglass? What happened to the person who invented the cotton gin, and the [African American] scientists, the artists?

These are the people I wanted to learn about. My people, and other people too. It wasn't just that I didn't learn about Blacks. I didn't learn about Asians, except that they built the train system. . . . I learned about Native Americans—Oh yeah, we killed a bunch of them, just so we could manifest our destiny. And so that really disturbed me growing up, and I guess that's part of the reason I got involved in Colors United when I came here, because that's one of our goals. We realize that we're in a setting where not everyone had the opportunity to learn about other people. And most of us come from homogeneous backgrounds—people dress the same as us, act the same, talk the same. And we don't know how to deal with others. We look at it as a burden, and actually, it's a great educational opportunity . . . and people should take advantage of that.

The seminar conversation moved from a discussion of racial stereotypes and misunderstanding to what would need to happen to move beyond these. Rev. Bailey suggested that college students can learn best by coming to the community and joining together in a successful and committed effort to help younger kids learn, and to help them develop a new sense of self worth and possibilities. Tracy then shared her own story of being part of an after-school tutoring program:

I'm a product of an after-school program in my home church. When I was five years old it was just a little room . . . in the back of our church. And now today I go home and they have a daycare center that's built across the street from the church, they have a full-fledged after-school program that's involved with the elementary school down the street. It has a community center that has lessons in karate, math, and science. They have firefighters who come in and volunteer, policemen who come volunteer, and it's all because people took an interest in the community and in their children. I've been a product of it, I see what it can do, and I want to give back. I want to share.

Around the seminar table the discussion evolved into what we could do as a college to work with and learn from the work that Rev. Bailey's community was doing to serve the interests of children and youth whose needs were not being met by the city schools. Rev. Bailey stressed the need for both White and Black students to get to know each other better, and the need for college students to take the risk to come to the community:

> You have to have [college] kids that just want to be different . . . kids who will go off campus, go to a service, spend some time. Look and see what people do. See what's affecting people's lives. Come and eat some good collard greens, some black-eyed peas, and some macaroni and cheese that's made homestyle, and some good fried chicken. I think that's what needs to happen.
>
> What we need are folk who are willing to be daring. I don't want people to come to Bethel who are pitying kids. I don't want people who think that they're going to some foreign country. Bethel has been in the community since 1816. So it's been in Lancaster longer than many of the other churches. People keep on acting like we just arrived. There are people who do not even know there are Black people in Lancaster, and we've been there since 1816.
>
> Our kids need to see that White folk are all right. Some of the teachers in the schools make you believe that White people are not all right. And some of the people who work in our community, because at five o'clock they're gone—even the church folk. And people see folk just leave—it's only Black and Latino after five o'clock. So they need to be able to see that not everybody's afraid of them. That they're not just some monster just waiting to drive by and shoot you all. They need to get to know some people.
>
> And that's the thing that's scary to me—that some of the kids are being raised who do not know anybody White. . . . They need to know that there are some people around who think differently, who look differently, act differently. And I'm not afraid of them.

In describing the tutoring program begun by Mrs. Davis, Rev. Bailey explained why they have been successful with students:

> What we're trying to do in Lancaster is to give them an atmosphere that encourages them to learn. The kids know Mrs. Davis

cares about them, and because of that they will come. We've seen kids who were not reading who are reading. We've seen parents who were not involved in the kids' homework starting to get involved. Sometimes forty or fifty kids come. . . . And what's happening is that learning is becoming accepted.

Because quite contrary to what people believe, it's not the home that doesn't believe that children should learn in the Black Community, nor the Latino Community. It's the school. Once you get through that it's okay, by an authority figure, to want to learn—it's okay to move yourself ahead in life, it's fine, it's what you're supposed to do—you'd be surprised how quickly they learn.

If you expect something of people, you will get it. If you expect them to be dumb, that's what they're going to be. If you expect them to be able to learn, they will learn.

At the end of the evening seminar, Rev. Bailey invited the students to come to visit in the community, share a meal, and meet with Mrs. Davis and other community members. Over the three months that followed there were a number of visits between the Bethel AME community and students, faculty, and administration from the college to share ideas and visions, and to plan for a mutually beneficial partnership.

The organizing team from the college included the social work chair, Dr. Vivian Bergel, and myself from the education department, the social work and education honor societies (Crystal Martin, president of Phi Alpha; Jason Berkenstock and Nathan Troutman of Kappa Delta Pi), and Tracy Jackson from Colors United. Together with Rev. Bailey and Mrs. Davis, they made plans to begin the tutoring partnership on February 8, 1998. The four student organizers took the lead, recruiting and organizing thirty-five college students to make the one-and-one-half-hour round trip to Lancaster on Monday and Thursday to tutor from 5 to 6:30 P.M. throughout the semester.

Once a month students organized a community dinner in Lancaster so that the tutors, their students, and other community members could talk together and continue to build and improve the partnership project. At the end of the semester there was a visit to the college campus by the Bethel AME students and their families. The tutoring project was supported the second year by our college president, Dr. Theodore Long, with a President's Fund for Distinction grant, providing funds for student transportation, multicultural literature, nonfiction books and materials, and three computers and programs.

Student Response to the Partnership

When my college students began the partnership in the 1998 spring semester, many of them had never attended an African American church service or spent any time in an African American community. They were impressed with the warmth, energy, and commitment that they saw within the community, and they were amazed at the love and care with which community members supported and encouraged the youth as they sang or spoke in the service.

Adults too were affirmed as they spoke or sang or prayed in an engaging call-and-response dialogue that created a strong sense of community involvement and mutual support. Mrs. Davis described the service to me as a sanctuary where you can learn to handle life outside, which is not always affirming and supportive, reminding me again of the lyrics "And let all who toil, let them come to the water . . ."

So we began the tutoring project with a two-and-one-half-hour church service—usual for the church community, but not for my college students. Afterward the students joined the Bethel AME community at their Cultural Center to share a delicious soul food meal and have an informal orientation to the tutoring program. Here are some of the dialogue-journal responses and classroom discussion comments of my students after this experience:

- Wow! This is the first word that comes to my mind. . . . Walking into the church, I had no idea what to expect. By the end of the service I felt that my faith had been renewed. I am not talking [about] just the spiritual sense (meaning the Bible and God). I have found a true sense of community, compassion, dedication, and sincerity. This community is bonded around the belief that they can make a difference in the world.

- I'll admit that I was intimidated when I walked in at first. Yet, it wasn't long before the service started and I got warm smiles and welcomes from those seated around me. . . . I was so surprised that they wanted us to belong to their community. I guess I thought we would just observe or watch their service, have dinner, find out who we were going to be teaching, and then go home. Was I wrong!

- I felt a part of the service that I thought I was just going to be observing. These people were so accepting [of] our presence. They could just as easily have turned us away and gone in search of African American college students. Instead, they put aside their ideas of the stereotypes . . . and gave us a chance to make a difference to help children to learn. Not to help Blacks to learn or to pity impoverished children, but to sit down with a student and help them get one step closer to becoming successful.

- Afterwards at the luncheon they wanted to know what each of us thought. They could have just all left and done what they needed to do. But I got so many hugs from people. And so many people wanted to share experiences with us, and ask us questions about what we were doing. They're just really interested in all aspects of our lives, and not just what we can do for them.

- Going into the inner city and tutoring was out of my comfort zone. But it just seemed that their eagerness—the kids that were there were very eager for us to come in. And that just makes me more eager and more comfortable with it, just knowing that I think I'm going to learn a lot more from them, and in turn expand myself.

All thirty-five of the college students who began tutoring returned faithfully each week. Social work, education, and occupational therapy students were particularly grateful for the experience, but students from other disciplines appreciated it too. After a semester of weekly tutoring at the Cultural Center, students responded in questionnaires, journals, and final reflection papers about the impact of this experience on them. A senior in psychology wrote:

> I think I truly found myself happy when I was at the Bethel AME Church. I was there as a minority, and at first it was an uncomfortable feeling. But then I thought, "This is something they have to deal with much more often than I do. If they don't have a problem with me, then I shouldn't have a problem with myself." It made me very empathetic to what they must experience.

A senior in occupational therapy wrote:

> I am glad that I got the opportunity before I graduate to be exposed to different cultures at the African Methodist Episcopal Church in Lancaster. . . . Hopefully I can take this new knowledge into the clinic and incorporate it into my therapeutic plan. . . . I learned the importance of celebrating a patient's culture and using it in therapy to ensure a positive experience for both patient and therapist.

One student could not attend the church service when we went as a group, so she attended by herself a few weeks later. Her experience as the only White person in the church summarizes well what students have learned from visiting the Bethel AME community, and the amazing love and care that makes this community so special.

Amy arrived at the church at 11 A.M., unaware of the length of the service. After nearly two hours she finally asked an older woman next to her how long the service lasted. The woman asked her if she had eaten breakfast, and Amy said that she hadn't. The woman then got up and left the church. About twenty minutes later she returned, sat down beside Amy, opened her pocketbook, and handed Amy a sandwich. Then, after the service, Amy was greeted with many hugs and warm welcomes by other Bethel AME community members.

Dealing with Race in School

Until the Ku Klux Klan came to my hometown of Carlisle, Pennsylvania, in the fall of 2000, the town and school district were in a state of denial about race problems and the need for an anti-bias curriculum in the schools. The Klan's visit to speak on the courthouse steps was a wake-up call.

The winter 1998 issue of the *Intelligence Report,* published by the Southern Poverty Law Center, reported that "474 Hate Groups Blanket America." By 1999 this number grew to over 500. Only three other states in the country have more active hate groups than our state of Pennsylvania.

In a community dialogue on racism in schools sponsored by the YWCA's Social Justice Committee, high school students from Carlisle described the way the system works in their small town. They described their perception that Lamberton Middle School houses mostly upper-class White students, while the majority of Black students attend Wilson Middle School. Also, most of the students in the high school honors courses are White and attended "upscale" schools such as Mooreland Elementary.

Jenel Browne tearfully described being the only Black student in her academically advanced courses: "I used to dread student assemblies. I would have to walk past the Blacks and they'd call me 'White.' And I'd sit with the Whites and I felt like I didn't belong there either." Jenel's mother, Sonia Browne, a previous president of the Social Justice Committee and a leader in her own community, used to pray with her daughter every morning before school to help her get through the day.

Nya Frohman recounted how one of her elementary school friends called her "Jew" at school during an argument, and stopped playing with her when she found out that Nya was Jewish. Jamica Browne, Jenel's sister, told of her experiences in elementary school where a peer continually called her "nigger." Jamica didn't retaliate with hatred, however, because her mother told her, "You can't fight ignorance with ignorance."

Collaboration: How We *Can* All Get Along

It is not "new" news that we live in a competitive and individualistic society. Our schools teach competition through individual testing, which leads to individual labels, tracks, and unequal (or denied) opportunities (Coles 1998; Taylor 1991; Bartoli 1995). Our profit-focused workplaces enforce competition. And our political system relies on electoral competition. Many will argue that this is as it should be: that we need competition to advance as a society. Many politicians suggest even more of the same for education: more testing of children, more competition between schools, more testing of teachers, "merit" pay to reward high test scores, and more school choice with vouchers and charter schools to increase competition.

As college social work and education faculty, and as participants in state and national education and human services dialogues, many of us find ourselves particularly in conflict with competitive policies and marketplace viewpoints that we believe to be harmful to children and to the future of democratic teaching and learning. This includes the harmful overuse and reliance on standardized testing for young children, the use of deficit labels that accompany the tests, and the unequal distribution of rewards and resources to those who compete well on tests.

This also includes the harmful effects of low expectations and unexamined race, culture, and class biases that often underlie the low expectations for success in learning and the failure of students of color. And it includes textbook-bound teaching and other limiting practices that reduce the full range of access to knowledge for all learners, deny opportunities for critical thinking in the classroom, and constrain a re-thinking of the entire educational system that could lead to more equitable and excellent learning for all students.

But the conflicts we fall into and the oppositional way in which we approach needed change have become part of the entrenched problem. So when we see what appears to be uninformed or biased teaching or policymaking, we are inclined to label this as bad, and to resist or ignore the offending teacher/administrator/department chair/secretary of education. We resign ourselves to a view of them as illiterate and impossible to change, hoping that they are ultimately discredited, denied tenure, gotten out of a position of influence or power, or retired.

We (and I include myself in this "we") really do not want to do the hard work of building respectful and collaborative relationships across differences, supporting the growth of those we are in opposition with, and celebrating their strengths. But indeed, I think that this is the only way—the long hard road to respectful relationship-building, mutual support, and learning to get along with each other. Sonia Browne had it right: "You can't fight ignorance with ignorance." And you certainly can't teach tolerance with intolerance.

Resources for Teaching Collaboration

The Southern Poverty Law Center, spearheaded by Morris Dees, makes an attempt to "teach tolerance" in their magazine of that name. They have published a number of excellent videos and books (such as *Starting Small: Teaching Tolerance in Preschool and the Early Grades, A History of Intolerance, Fighting Hate in School*) for classroom teachers and schools, along with other excellent materials on fighting hate in school. They also publish information in their periodical, *Intelligence Report,* about human rights abuses, current updates on hate groups, and new materials for teachers. Their community response guide, *Ten Ways to Fight Hate,* is another of their fine resources (see www.spl.org).

All of the major education associations have excellent materials for multicultural and anti-racist teaching. NAEYC's book, *Anti-Bias Curriculum,* by Louise Derman Sparks, is an excellent resource for teaching young children. Other teachers associations (NCTE for English and language arts, IRA for reading, NCSS for social studies) as well as NASW for social work publish very good materials for teaching about diversity and racism.

Rethinking Schools, an urban education periodical edited by Bob Peterson and other fine progressive educators, is an excellent resource for teachers (see www.rethinkingschools.org). There are entire issues on Ebonics, bilingual education, and testing; and they publish bibliographies of books by and about Native Americans, African Americans, Asian Americans, Puerto Ricans, Mexicans, and literature from many other cultures and nationalities. The National Coalition of Education

Activists is another source for ideas, workshops, and excellent materials to build a diverse classroom curriculum.

The *Teaching for Change* catalog from the Network of Educators on the Americas carries a wide assortment of excellent anti-racist and multicultural books, including *Beyond Heroes and Holidays* by Enid Lee, Deborah Menkart, and Margo Okazawa-Rey; and Beverly Tatum's *Why Are All the Black Kids Sitting Together in the Cafeteria?*

Fortunately, a growing number of educators in multicultural and anti-racist education are publishing books, book lists, activities, and other teaching materials. And these support teachers in their efforts to make themselves and their students more knowledgeable about cultures and races different from their own in an effort to promote more understanding, tolerance, and celebration of diversity. In addition to the sources listed above, two books that are highly recommended are *Teaching/Learning Anti-Racism* (Derman-Sparks and Phillips 1997) and *Opening Minds to Equality* (Schniedewind and Davidson 1998).

Staying Hopeful

> *All the other parts of the earth's life seem to get along, to fit in with each other, to accommodate, even to concede when the stakes are high. . . . We [humans] are the anomalies for the moment, the self-conscious children at the edge of the crowd, unsure of our place, unwilling to join up, tending to grabbiness*
> —LEWIS THOMAS

If we can develop more college courses with urban field experiences, and if we can engage in collaborative, respectful service learning in richly diverse sites, I believe we really can learn to get along—even across our entrenched race and class divides. Experiences in multiracial sites encourage reflection on personal assumptions and biases as well as understanding and appreciation of others. This kind of community-based experiential learning is important for all citizens in a pluralistic democracy, but it is particularly vital for teacher preparation in the twenty-first century.

Camille Hopkins, an excellent city teacher from Martin Luther King Elementary School in Lancaster, told me recently that her urban education class and placement at the Martin Luther King school were what convinced her to teach there. For Erick Valentin and Elizabeth

Wisegarver, two of my previous students who are now city teachers, it was the experience of student teaching in Lancaster that sealed their decision to be city teachers.

But do these courses "work"? Perhaps the best way to answer this question is to let the students speak for themselves. It would be too idealistic to suggest that we can reach everyone through a collaborative reading, experiencing, listening, thinking, writing, and talking process—especially in only one or two semesters. But in the majority of the journals, research papers, and semester reflection papers from my courses in urban issues, urban education, and celebrating diversity in a democracy, students expressed a deeper understanding of race issues, and a greater appreciation for diversity. Here are a few of their comments:

- After completing my independent research, my opinions on socioeconomic issues have changed drastically. As I ran through a list of topics that dealt with both diversity and my future career as a social worker, it seemed as if they were all interconnected. After pondering what the connecting factor was, I came to realize what a problem poverty is. Before I began this research I had no idea as to the real numbers of people who live in poverty or with an income so low that providing essentials for the family strains the budget.

- The most important thing this class has taught me is to keep an open mind and to be willing to listen to someone else's opinion if it differs from my own, and to consider their reasons for holding that opinion.

- This class has shown me what learning is all about. We would be left to do work regarding a topic of our choice, and then forced to develop our own ideas and beliefs from that. It was scary at times. I was forced to sit down and search within myself for how I felt about racism, prejudices, welfare and the poverty issues, gender roles in our society along with numerous other topics. Every week I would learn something new about myself and about how our world worked.

- This class allowed me to explore my own identity while learning to appreciate the identity of others. By evaluating my own attitudes and beliefs concerning diversity, I came to the realization that I can truly make a difference in the welfare of others. By becoming an advocate for diversity issues, I can continue to spread the message regarding the importance of celebrating individual differences in everyday life.

- I think we all need to realize that acceptance of diversity is the greatest gift we could give ourselves. Only when we all learn to accept the differences among ourselves, will we be able to accept who we really are as our own personal self.

But, unfortunately, you can't win them all. There were several students in each class who were very unhappy, and they voiced their frustration and anger on student evaluation forms or complaints to others. One very dissatisfied student, who refused to visit the Bethel AME Church or Cultural Center, and who adamantly refused to do service learning in a diverse site, commented in her course evaluation:

- I think this course is an oxymoron in itself. The course is about diversity yet we were all supposed to think the same on the issues. We were not encouraged to think for ourselves—no, excuse me. We were encouraged to think for ourselves but then we were punished, put down, told to think with an open mind.

Other students felt overworked, frustrated, and disappointed:

- I was disappointed with this class. I expected that we would discuss other differences other than racial- and gender-related ones.

- At times the work seemed a bit overwhelming. I was accustomed to having a very structured, definite set of work that needed to be accomplished. I think the overall frustration came from the fact that no one was used to having this kind of class. However, beneath all of the confusion, I did learn a lot about myself and others. Thanks.

- I feel there was too much work for this being a core class. Cut back on community service hours, because this is not the only class we have. Find more diversity. We only focused on poor Blacks and homeless people.

On the Future of Our Pluralistic Democracy

How can new teachers, the majority of whom are White and monolingual, be prepared to teach successfully in the multiracial, multilingual classrooms of the future? And how can this happen in majority White, monolingual teacher-education programs? These are central questions for the future of our democratic experiment in education—ones that may determine the success or failure of our great American goals of equality and justice for all citizens.

As we look ahead to the richly diverse classrooms of the twenty-first century, populated with a minimum of 40 percent students of color, we also face a growing shortage of new teachers of color—less than 5 percent in recent surveys. For educators, this leads to the critical issue of learning to teach across race, culture, and language. We have historically done very poorly with this, and the experience of far too many African American and Latino students has been one of victim blaming (Kozol 1992), targeting for labels of deficit or behavior problems (Bartoli and Botel 1988; Bartoli 1995), or invisibility through misunderstanding or neglect (Kuykendahl 1992; Fordham 1990; Tatum 1998).

The National Council of Teachers of English Commission on Teacher Education for Teachers of Urban, Rural, and Suburban Students of Color worked together for five years on these issues and questions. We took seriously Lisa Delpit's (1995) cautions about teaching other people's children, and Peggy McIntosh's (1989) research on "White Privilege" that cites the limits of our own understanding of building respectful relationships across race and culture. After much discussion, debate, and sharing of drafts, Dawn Abt-Perkins and Lois Matz Rosen outlined four principles that provide a framework for teacher education in multicultural literacy. In much abbreviated form, these are:

1. Teachers' awareness of their own cultural values, beliefs, and assumptions is central in understanding the actions, voices, and texts of students of color in the classroom.

2. "Culture-free," color-blind, or acritical approaches to teaching are not justifiable: teachers need to understand the values and potential effects of their practice on students of color.

3. Teachers should be prepared to help students discover and explore their own ethnic connections and affirm their own cultural identity.

4. A primary focus of teacher-education programs should be to develop the attitudes and understandings that lead to effective literacy teaching in multicultural and multiracial classrooms, building attitudes of openness and acceptance of diversity in language, culture, and race in their classrooms.

This framework goes beyond electives, concentrations, or other add-ons to a fundamental reframing of the entire teacher-preparation program, focusing on celebrating the rich promise of diversity in a pluralistic democracy.

A Final Note on Staying in the Struggle

If indeed "all the other parts of the earth's life seem to get along, to fit in with each other, to accommodate," then perhaps we have a broader ecological role model for getting along. Lewis Thomas (1992) is optimistic about our fragile, adolescent human species:

> Growing up is hard times for an individual but sustained torment for a whole species, especially one as brainy and nervous as ours. If we can last it out, get through the phase, shake off the memory of this century, wait for a break, we may find ourselves off and running again. (25)

As a final note on the possibilities of getting along, I must add that, when circumstances are their most difficult and seemingly impossible, I am particularly inspired by the persistent goodwill and faith of my Bethel AME colleagues, Wanda Davis and Rev. Edward Bailey; my social work colleague, Vivian Bergel; my Carlisle colleague, Shelli Palmer Felton; Cheri Honkala and members of the Kensington Welfare Rights Union in Philadelphia; and, of course, all of the amazing city teachers whom I have been fortunate enough to meet.

Their vision, courage, enthusiasm, commitment, and persistence amid seemingly impossible conditions, circumstances, and events inspire me to continue and to stay in the struggle. But the final word on this must go to Frederick Douglass, who wrote in 1856 about the value of adversity and the need to continue the struggle for both equality and educational excellence:

> If there is no struggle, there is no progress. Those who profess to favor freedom and yet deprecate agitation are people who want crops without plowing the ground. They want rain without thunder and lightning. That struggle might be a moral one; it might be a physical one; it might be both moral and physical, but it must be a struggle. Power concedes nothing without a demand. It never did and never will.

REFLECTION: WHAT STOOD OUT FOR ME?

☐ Reframing teacher education with a primary focus on deeper understanding and support of students from all racial, cultural, and economic backgrounds is vital for the future of our democracy.

☐ College courses linked with meaningful experiences in urban communities are important for unlearning racial, cultural, and economic stereotypes.

☐ We have much to learn from the committed work of urban community members, and partnering with them can help college students to learn about civic responsibility and transformative change.

☐ We humans *can* all learn to get along, just like the rest of the species in our ecology.

7
What Can I Do?

The stories in this book—about city teachers, their schools, and their communities—are not so much stories of individual heroism as they are stories of collective struggle and collaborative resistance. Although I am genuinely in awe of the teachers, teacher leaders, parents, and community leaders whom I have come to know and to deeply respect, to only celebrate them as individuals would miss the power of the complex ecology for learning that they have created together. And it would miss the model that they provide us for collaboratively transforming urban education, and, in fact, all education.

A guiding question throughout my research, analysis, and writing about successful city teachers and their schools has been, "Why don't we have more of these? Why can't we replicate these models?" Seymour Sarason asked me this question four years ago, and I have been struggling to answer it ever since. I believe that there are a number of interconnected reasons why we do not have more elementary schools like Taylor, Harrington, Central Park East II, and PS 114.

One reason for these models not spreading is the illiteracy of our most literate policymakers (a phrase coined by Morton Botel), and the accompanying problem of the shortsighted, misinformed policies that they create.

But it is not policymakers alone who are illiterate about literacy and caring for all of our children—it is the general public as well. As Valerie Polakow (2000) powerfully reminds us, we are witnessing a *Public Assault on America's Children*. The lack of critical and reflective thinking about meaningful education, child poverty, racism, juvenile injustice, democracy, and the common good on the part of citizens in the United States should cause us all to worry about the future of education in a democracy. We may be seeing the end result of an education system that is based on trivial pursuits: on one-right-answer approaches rather than serious critical thinking and complex problem solving that demands respect for multiple points of view.

The passive acceptance by the general public of half-truths about education, and the acceptance of social policies that criminalize the poor, are alarming trends. Likewise for the lack of a societal commitment to the common good. A democracy cannot survive without a critically thinking citizenry, able to weigh competing evidence and make well-informed choices. Neither can it survive with a widening gap between the rich and the poor, between children of color and white children, and a digital divide that follows the same color line.

So what can we do? The short answer to Seymour Sarason's question (Why don't we have more of these [successful city schools]?) is that, as a society, we haven't made a unified commitment to the common good; nor have we done the necessary organizing, planning, and ecologically informed policymaking to ensure that all of our children have a life that is free from the violence of poverty. And that is essentially why we have the highest child poverty rate in the industrialized world, and why we invest the least in reducing that abysmal rate (see Figure 7–1).

I believe that the examples provided by the teachers and parents at Taylor, Harrington, Central Park East II, PS 114, the Bethel AME community, and the Kensington Welfare Rights Union provide us with excellent models for a collaborative struggle for change. And their models are in the rich tradition of our democratic history of collective resistance to inequality, poverty, and injustice, suggesting the value of:

- a lifetime dedication to educating all children, even in the face of inequality and poverty
- continual growth and learning as professionals, and administrative support for that growth
- a commitment to each other as colleagues in developing a collaborative family environment, both in and out of school
- mutual respect, trust, and support that is shared among teachers and parents in a united effort to care for and educate each child
- including and celebrating the language and culture of the children and families in the community
- evaluation methods that document strengths, potential, and continual growth
- staying in the struggle to eliminate racism, injustice, and inequality

Child Poverty in Industrial Countries

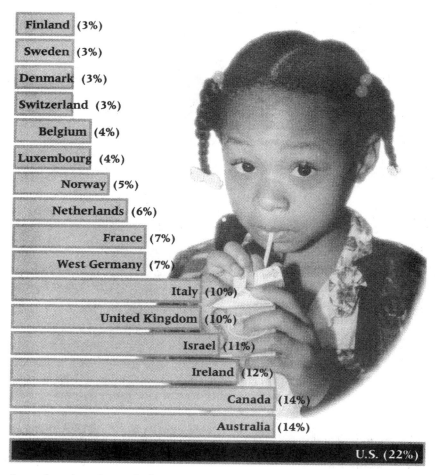

Finland (3%)

Sweden (3%)

Denmark (3%)

Switzerland (3%)

Belgium (4%)

Luxembourg (4%)

Norway (5%)

Netherlands (6%)

France (7%)

West Germany (7%)

Italy (10%)

United Kingdom (10%)

Israel (11%)

Ireland (12%)

Canada (14%)

Australia (14%)

U.S. (22%)

Source: Luxembourg Income Study
Figure 7–1A.

All of this, and more, is what education in a democracy is all about.

But rather than standing back in awe of these teachers, parents, and community members, we need to join with them in support of what they are striving so hard to do. So this chapter offers suggestions on what we can each do—as teachers and school leaders, as parents and community members, as college students, as policymakers, and as concerned citizens in a democracy.

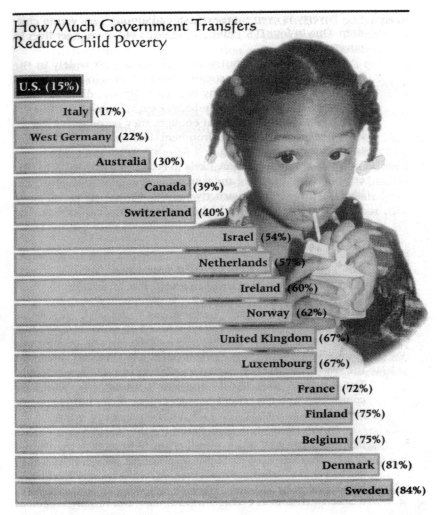

How Much Government Transfers
Reduce Child Poverty

U.S. (15%)
Italy (17%)
West Germany (22%)
Australia (30%)
Canada (39%)
Switzerland (40%)
Israel (54%)
Netherlands (57%)
Ireland (60%)
Norway (62%)
United Kingdom (67%)
Luxembourg (67%)
France (72%)
Finland (75%)
Belgium (75%)
Denmark (81%)
Sweden (84%)

Source: Luxembourg Income Study
Figure 7–1B.

What Can I Do as a Teacher and Teacher Leader?

We need teachers as never before to educate not only our students, but to educate the public and the policymakers. All citizens and policymakers need to know about and to critically understand:

- **The importance of respecting and supporting the professional knowledge and experience of teachers.** Only teachers in the classroom on a day-to-day basis can validly and knowledgeably evaluate the growth of their students. Continuous observation and documentation of learning by teachers and support staff, combined with student self-evaluation and the collaboration of peers and family, provide a full, accurate, and valid evaluation of the growth and development of learners. In addition, the processes of observation, documentation, self-evaluation, and collaborative review increase the knowledge, abilities, and critical thinking of all who are involved.

- **The importance of adequate and equitable funding for all schools in all communities.** There is no excuse for "savage inequalities" and unequal opportunities in a democracy. The evidence is clear that better-funded and better-resourced schools are more able to provide equal opportunity for all students, regardless of the income of their families.

- **The violence of poverty and its devastating effect on the potentials of poor urban children and families.** *The State of America's Children, 2000* and other resources from the Children's Defense Fund along with publications from Bread for the World and other nonprofit organizations give accurate and truthful information on the plight of the thirty-five million U.S. citizens who live in poverty, the majority of whom are children.

- **The effects of ill-informed and mean-spirited public policies,** such as welfare "reform," that further diminish the life chances of children and families who are impoverished and living in despair and desperation (Polakow 2000; Beckmann and Simon 1999; Sider 2000).

- **The dangers, the inequalities, the abuse to children and teachers, and ultimately the violence of high-stakes, standardized testing practices.** Excellent resources for fully understanding this are available, such as Alfie Kohn's (2000) *The Case Against Standardized Testing*, Linda McNeil's (2000) *Contradictions of School Reform*, Kathy Swope and Barbara Miner's (2000) *Failing Our Kids: Why the Testing Craze Won't Fix Our Schools*, Monty Neil's research and resources at www.fairtest.org, and a variety of the *Rethinking Schools* issues listed at www.rethinkingschools.org.

- **The vital importance of creating ecologically sensitive public policies** that support and maintain present and future school environments of cooperation, trust, mutual respect, and mutual support.

- **The importance of good, public, nonsegregated preschools for all children.** At present the United States has the most racially and economically segregated preschools in the world, and this segregation is replicated in our alarmingly growing prison population.
- **The importance of providing good social and medical services for children and families in poor urban communities.**

And where will teachers learn to do all of this educating of the public, in addition to their already heavy demands in educating the students in the classroom? Ideally, they would learn about this in transformed colleges of education that have a vision and mission that matches the best of our democratic and civic ideals. And this is why Seymour Sarason places such a great emphasis on transforming teacher education.

What Can I Do as a Teacher Educator?

We know that the student population in U.S. classrooms will soon be 40 percent children of color—even in the suburbs—while the teaching population is 95 percent white. So there is a vital need for teacher-preparation programs that help white teachers gain the cross-cultural knowledge that will ensure the success of all of their students.

I spoke with Seymour Sarason recently about some of the challenges for teacher-preparation programs in the United States. He noted that presently it is not unusual for teachers to have their practicums and student-teaching experiences in schools that have little or no relationship to the schools that I have described in this book. Yet it is the teachers in these city schools who have found the ways to use themselves, their students and families, their teaching colleagues, and others as resources for making a difference in the lives of urban children and youth. In Seymour Sarason's words, they have "redefined what a resource is" (2000).

So one way to prepare new city teachers is to place them in the classrooms of good urban teachers so that they can learn what they need to know about working successfully with children of color and relating in respectful and supportive ways to their families. In addition, because White middle-class teacher-education students have been socialized in a certain way—Beverly Tatum (1998) calls it breathing in the "smog" of racism, which is the only air around to breathe—it is vital to unlearn some of their prior learning of biases and stereotypes.

Reverend Edward Bailey and I talked about the need to develop teachers who care: teachers who are sensitive to the enormous effects of poverty and racism on children's motivation, learning, and growth. How will we teach teachers to care in the way that Wanda Davis cares for the children in the Bethel AME tutoring program? How will we develop teachers who can reflect upon their own white privileges, and their culturally learned heritage of stereotypes and biases, like Wendy Shapiro asked the Taylor teachers to do? How will we prepare teachers who can celebrate the language and culture of their students the way that Teresa Alvarez, Diana Diaz, Debbie Williams, and Linda Kidd do throughout the year in their classrooms? How will we prepare teachers who can relate to children, parents, and communities who are culturally and racially different from them?

At a minimum, this reflective and transformative teacher education requires:

1. serious reflection on one's own assumptions and biases concerning race, class, and language

2. multiple opportunities to work with students of color and their families in respectful and collaborative ways

3. multiple opportunities to observe and to practice teach in racially diverse classrooms and schools

4. required college courses that explore multicultural and anti-racist education, including all of the racial and linguistic issues that are a part of this, such as bilingual education, Ebonics, English as a second language, teaching for social justice, and celebrating diversity as a rich resource in and out of the classroom

5. required college courses that include the rich multicultural literature and history that more fully represents our pluralistic democracy

6. successful strategies for working together respectfully and supportively with students and parents in racially diverse communities

Teachers can also learn some of this in public schools where the faculty works and learns together in a continuous, reflective, mutually supportive way. The staff development at Taylor, Harrington, Central Park East II, and PS 114 provides good examples of continuous professional development and the creation of school ecologies of cooperation, trust, and mutual respect.

The partnership of a college or university with city schools and the development of professional development schools make it possible for K–12 public school and college teachers and students to work together in mutually beneficial ways. Together they can mentor the next generation of transformative teachers, capable of critical reflection and able to inform the public on education policies, supportive services, and equitable opportunities for all learners. It is a tragedy of our democracy that this mission has not been fully embraced by all teacher-preparation programs.

What Can I Do as a Parent and Community Member?

Knowledgeable parents and community members need to educate fellow parents and community members about what makes education truly meaningful and successful, what supports high-quality teaching and learning, and what is politically driven and potentially harmful to their children. We need to learn all that we can as parents about how to work collaboratively with teachers and schools in support of what is best for our children.

We can become more informed and knowledgeable about successful teaching and learning through the publications of numerous education associations (NCTE, IRA, NCSS, AERA, NCTM, NCST, NAEYC, Phi Delta Kappa, Kappa Delta Pi) and organizations (Children's Defense Fund, Fairtest, Rethinking Schools, National Coalition of Education Activists). The Taylor Elementary School's parent organization, EPOP, and the PS 114 parents, who raised funds for classroom libraries and sewed twelve hundred book bags so their children could take a book home every night, provide good models for gathering resources and working together with the teachers and the school to enrich the reading program for their children.

It was parents from the Taylor School who researched and presented to the school the Reading Recovery program, originating in New Zealand, which has a 98 percent literacy rate. They also gathered information and visited another school to develop a Library Power program. And they initiated and organized a whole-school reading program that encouraged and motivated children to read dozens of extra books. Most importantly, the parents and community members worked collaboratively and respectfully with the teachers and school staff to share information, develop plans, and carry out those plans for the benefit of the children.

I asked JoBeth Allen her thoughts on ways that parents and teachers might build relationships with each other, drawing on the work she and her colleagues have done as collaborative action researchers. She shares here her insights gleaned from a decade of working among teachers, families, and children in Georgia:

> I would love to sit down together with the outstanding city teachers Jill has portrayed in this book and the outstanding rural, urban, and suburban teachers I have studied with in recent years. We have many parallel experiences, as well as much to learn from each other. Until that day when we might have a face-to-face dialogue, I'll imagine here how our ideas might intermingle in productive ways.
>
> When first-grade teacher Betty Shockley, second-grade teacher Barbara Michalove, and I studied the children we worried about most (Allen, Michalove, and Shockley 1993), we became acutely aware of how little we knew about the children's families, how little the families knew about what their children were doing in school, and how little genuine communication occurred. Betty designed, and Barbara adapted, a set of parallel practices to connect home and school literacy learning (Shockley, Michalove, and Allen 1995). They began with the parents' perspectives of their own children, inviting them to "Tell Me About Your Child" in writing at the beginning of each year. Parents in this low-income, predominantly African American neighborhood poured out their hopes and humor, information and insights, advice and anxieties about what their children were like, and what they hoped school would be like for their children. Teachers and families kept this dialogue going all year in journals the children took home two to three times a week.
>
> Parents or others in the family sustained a remarkable commitment to read with their children, talk about the books, and write together in the journals; Betty and Barbara honored their commitment by responding to every entry. This extended written communication, not about discipline problems or signing reading logs, established deep relationships. It also supported emerging readers and writers at home as well as at school in ways neither teacher nor parent could have accomplished alone.
>
> Other parallel practices of learning from families and connecting home and school literacy resonate with those of Debby Williams, Taylor School. Like Betty and Barbara, Debby sees parents as

her partners, and tells them what they can do to be her partner. But this is a respectful "training": she bases her curriculum on the belief that children bring a rich store of knowledge from home, that parents educate their children as much as she does. When parents come to meetings in her classroom, they know they will be talking about immediate concerns—what their children will be learning in the next month, what they can do to support that learning, not "ten things you should do to make your child a better reader." Most importantly, Debby lets the children know she cares, and when the child feels this, the parents know it and will support this person who values their child as they do.

Debbie Williams, at Harrington School, understands how important communication is—everything from contacting all families before school even begins to establish the yearlong partnership to the very language she uses. It is more informal, so as not to separate her from families—"Look, meet me the first day so I can let you know what I'm gonna be all about." Contrast this with the traditional Parent Night, a few weeks into school, when parents are herded into rooms to learn what supplies their children still haven't brought, and what rules their children just can't seem to follow (with the implicit message that parents obviously don't enforce these at home).

Building relationships with families means respecting them—their values, struggles, insights, culture, and language. Debbie can code switch, and she understands and values the Ebonics her children and their families speak at the same time that she helps them learn what Lisa Delpit calls Edited English, which is the cultural capital most will need for mainstream opportunities of advanced education and professional careers. Just as she understands, appreciates, and incorporates the children's rap music into her curriculum, showing children that it is connected with (not inferior to) other kinds of music including classical music, so she values Ebonics. This respectful stance builds bridges; children see their home—their family's—language as valid communication. Betty and Barbara demonstrated this respect by accepting both the content and form of whatever family members wrote in the journals; many of the writers for whom this type of correspondence was rare took great risks not only to write several times a week, but to contribute to family story books. These family stories were another way of bringing home cultures to the center of the classroom curriculum.

Similarly, when children and their parents see Diana Diaz and Teresa Alvarez's classrooms filled with artifacts of Puerto Rico, Nicaragua, and the Dominican Republic, they know that their home cultures are an honored and important part of schooling. Perhaps then it is easier to believe—to trust—that the other things the teachers select for study will also be valuable to their children. Culturally relevant teaching by definition makes connections between home and school cultures. It is enacted differently in every classroom. On an isolated island in Alaska, all ninety students and many of their parents and grandparents in the village of Tununak created the Yup'ik encyclopedia project, a bilingual, multimedia archive of tribal stories, knowledge, and skills that has engaged students in deep inquiry into the power of language in their changing society (Dyment 1997). In Teresa Alvarez's classroom, students connect with their family members who are still in Puerto Rico, writing to them in Spanish.

The Bethel AME tutoring project is an outstanding example of learning within the community. Jill's students have the opportunity to learn the rich "funds of knowledge" (Moll, Amanti, Neff, and Gonzales 1992) that families and children possess. Our current study group is trying to learn from children's photographs. The PhOLKS project (Photographs of Local Knowledge Sources) involves a diverse group of teachers (differing in age, experience, ethnicity, gender, and teaching assignments) working in culturally and economically diverse classrooms. Children photograph their out-of-school lives, dictate or write narratives of the pictures, and take the photographs home to have a family member write about them as well. We have learned a great deal about what the children value, what they like to do (and are good at) at home, and about their families. Parents seemed to relish the opportunity to talk about their children and their lives through the pictures, and they had control over the information they did and did not want shared.

Debbie, Debby, and others did not reach out to parents just to "increase parental involvement," a goal that is sometimes thought of in the very limited terms of parental trips to the school. They needed parents because they were valuable resources. Sixth-grade Bronx public school teacher Marceline Torres (1998) got her students involved in self-selected projects investigating "important questions and concerns about the world in which they live" (59) such as drugs, AIDS, teen pregnancy, and homelessness. She also got their parents involved, first by having students dialogue with their parents in "letters home," and second by holding monthly "celebrations" where students presented their research findings to their parents. Family members became valuable resources as, for example, one student interviewed his uncle who had AIDS and another got technical information about the disease from her father, who was an X-ray technician.

In LEADS (Literacy Education for a Democratic Society), a study group in Athens, Georgia, that met for four years (Allen 1999), several members included parents in their attempts to bring social justice issues to the forefront of their classrooms. Mollie Blackburn's (1999) students explored their own privilege as "gifted" students, drawing on many sources including their parents to explore social structures and attitudes about welfare, socioeconomic status, and social class. Barbara Michalove's (1999) fourth graders interviewed their parents about times they had personally experienced discrimination as part of an in-depth study of prejudice in the United States—and in their own classroom. Parents told her how important this inquiry was to their children, and how much they appreciated being called on to share their experiences.

We have much to learn from schools like Taylor Elementary that make school a truly welcoming place, where parents can walk into the school to deliver their children to the teacher, share pertinent information, and find out what they might need to be doing at home to support learning. Several years ago Betty (Shockley) Bisplinghoff and I were working with a group of teachers from Connecticut and New Jersey. We shared Jill's (Bartoli 1995) story about a largely Puerto Rican school in Philadelphia that had the twin problems of low parent involvement and parents who were coming into classrooms throughout the day (the school finally posted a sign that barred parents from entering the school).

Several teachers in the workshop were shocked—they recognized themselves. They set to work to build on the parental presence that before had seemed a nuisance. They opened the cafeteria to parents during the school breakfast program time, encouraged the parents to talk with teachers during this time, and had coffee and reading materials (newspapers and school newsletters) printed in both English and Spanish available for them to read. They made the school a truly welcoming place, and the school cafeteria a family dining room. And they began thinking of "parent involvement" in terms other than attendance at PTO meetings.

For any of these genuine invitations to develop into meaningful relationships, schools must invest the time and resources. We need principals like the one in this book who wisely addressed the need for phones in classrooms for calling parents and linking with social services. We need time—school time—to make home visits. We need supplies such as notebooks for home-school literacy journals, books for classroom libraries and for teacher study groups, and we need cameras and film for projects like PhOLKS. But most of all, we need the time and support to learn with parents, to listen carefully to their knowledge and concerns, and to talk with each other in order to develop culturally relevant curriculum that puts families at the center of learning.

What Can I Do as a College Student?

It was students at Elizabethtown College who took the leadership in beginning our tutoring and mentoring partnership with the Bethel AME Cultural Center and community. These students took the ideals of their organizations seriously: ideals like fidelity to humanity and service, from the social work and education honor societies, and appreciation of diversity from Colors United. And for the past three years it has been students who have driven the college vans to Lancaster twice a week, who have helped to organize the visit to the church and the community dinner, and who have developed the lists of tutors for each semester.

For our fall "Into the Streets" day, it has been students who have developed a Saturday service project at Bethel, recruited other students to help, gathered the materials, and arranged transportation. And when we have invited the students from Bethel to come to the college for a visit, it has been our college students who have organized the visit, served as tour guides, and taken the children to dinner with them.

Last semester students from Sara Sanders' social welfare issues class organized a "Family Holiday Celebration" at Martin Luther King Elementary School in Lancaster. There were 350 parents and children who came to create family holiday memory books, to which we added digital-camera pictures of each family. The families also learned more about Kwanzaa and Hanukkah traditions, they made a variety of holiday crafts together, and each family took home a children's book of their choice. During the same semester, a college student group called Students Investing in Free Enterprise (SIFE) organized a project at Bethel AME Cultural Center in which they engaged the youth in creating and marketing a product, giving them an opportunity to use their creative imaginations and get a taste for entrepreneurial business. The project also included hands-on math in a real-life, experiential context.

Other student-led projects have included organizing one thousand sandwiches for the KWRU Poor People's March for Economic Rights, which began in Philadelphia and ended at the United Nations in New York City. Students have also collected sleeping bags, blankets, coats, and other much-needed supplies for homeless and poor families in North Philadelphia.

A new student-led project this semester is a pen-pal letter exchange with the fifth-grade classes at Martin Luther King School. First-year college students have recruited sixty fellow students for this project. College students will also be hosting on campus the Peace-makers Club—a group of seventy fourth and fifth graders from M. L. King who have been studying mediation, nonviolence, and peace making with their inspiring social skills teacher, Frank Albrecht.

In short, college students can (1) organize service-learning programs and projects connected with urban schools and communities, and (2) collaborate and organize with other student groups on campus to raise awareness and to develop long-term service learning projects in urban communities and schools.

There are many ways that experiential learning and working together with urban communities can enrich students' academic learning. This semester there are four professors whose courses in social work, occupational therapy, and urban issues will include placements at Bethel and M. L. King. The field experiences will enrich the academic courses, providing context-rich experiences and opportunities for serious reflection on the major issues in each course.

With these kinds of experiences, students are more invested in doing research on such issues as homelessness, juvenile injustice, child poverty, and urban education. Within their various disciplines they can research inequalities in social policy, health services, and school funding. And they can take this research to the advocacy level by joining together with such advocacy groups as KWRU, the Underground Railroad (a social work group in North Philadelphia), Bread for the

World, Partnerships for Children, and many other advocates for the rights of poor children and families.

College students can, in short, go out and make a difference: leave campus and go into city schools and communities to work together with parents, teachers, and community members who care about the rights of poor children and their families. They can make a difference in the lives of children and youth by advocating for the support of schools and families in poor urban communities.

What Can I Do as a Policymaker and a Citizen in a Democracy?

The first and most important thing for policymakers and all citizens to do is to get fully and accurately informed—get literate on current education and social policy research that is well grounded and unbiased. For instance, it is illiterate to assume that testing children will improve their learning: it's like assuming that taking a person's temperature more often or taking more X-rays will improve their health. More enriched opportunities to learn, better conditions and resources for learning, more support for teacher professional development, surrounding children with personally meaningful and engaging books and other excellent learning materials, and attending to children's social, emotional, physical, economic, intellectual, and spiritual needs will improve learning.

Imagine the fallacy of having a group of psychologists devise a test to measure people as ministers, parents, senators, or governors. Then imagine forcing all clergy, parents, and elected officials to take these tests and publishing the scores in every newspaper across the country. How long do you think it would take for the protests:

> Whose definition of a "good" parent are you using?
>
> Why didn't you talk with/work together with us in the ministry in devising the test?
>
> How can any one test measure my ability as a senator?
>
> You have to observe me working with people to evaluate what I can really do.

The same fallacy exists in the testing of students and the testing of teachers as the answer to improving education. Decontextualized and ecologically invalid tests are a weak substitute for careful, informed, contextually grounded observation and documentation of the ongoing teaching and learning processes. And not involving the student and teacher in the process of documentation and self-evaluation is both disrespectful and disempowering, contradicting the very purpose of education in a democracy.

If our aim in education is critical thinking, rather than rote learning, learners must be engaged in the self-reflection and evaluation process. They must be empowered as authors of their own learning, not the disempowered objects of the opinions and viewpoints of distant others.

It is equally illiterate to assume that welfare "reform" as it is presently being implemented will eliminate the poverty of city children and the joblessness of their parents. More meaningful living-wage jobs in urban communities will eliminate joblessness; and giving economic support to those who are living in poverty will eliminate poverty. Every other country in the industrialized world has been able to do this, thereby drastically reducing the child poverty in their countries (see Figure 7–1A and B, pages 119–120). Similarly, more affordable and accessible housing and health care (rather than transplanting, temporarily sheltering, fining, or imprisoning those who are left destitute) will help to eliminate homelessness.

In 1999 Mayor Rendell reported that there were fifty-five thousand people in Philadelphia who needed jobs, but only fifteen thousand jobs were available. Yet welfare reform policies insist that poor mothers find nonexistent jobs and get nonexistent child care for their children, while they put in twenty hours or more at a low-wage job that requires hours of travel to malls outside the city, and that provides no health care for their family. Little mention is made in welfare reform policies of the millions of poor children who are being deprived of the care of their mothers. Similarly, in the rush to put poor women to work, there is little mention that 50 percent of the women who are homeless are fleeing from abusive spouses. Forced labor and motherless children are the products of welfare "reform."

Getting Informed About Education and Public Policy

Research on education from the major education associations that represent teachers at all levels (see "What Can I Do as a Parent and Community Member?") is vital. Gerald Coles (2000), Denny Taylor (1996), and Richard Allington (1998) have documented the ways that research on reading has been manipulated, distorted, and misused for political and profit motives, with the end result of poor readers getting poorer while commercial textbook and test publishers and other profiteers get richer. Sadly, there is an abundance of decontextualized, shallow, and biased research in the field of education, which makes it even harder for policymakers and the public to know what to believe.

Thus, equally important as critical reading of the research is respecting the professional knowledge and experience of dedicated and committed teachers, and making sure that the voices of good teachers are heard in the policymaking process. If we want intelligent, informed, and successful health and wellness policies, we should not exclude the voices of health-care professionals. Education policies, however, often exclude the voices of those who know the most about supporting the learning of their students—those who are most qualified to debunk invalid, incomplete, or ill-conceived research about the teaching, learning, and evaluation processes.

City teachers understand the absurdity of reducing the curriculum to test-taking skills. They, like McNeil (2000), see the enormous amounts of time and money wasted on testing and preparation for tests that deprive city children of the opportunities to learn in meaningful and lasting ways. Community members and policymakers need to hear the voices of these teachers.

As an example, I sat recently in the faculty lunchroom with a group of teachers at Martin Luther King Elementary School in Lancaster. They had a clear sense of what is needed to truly transform city schools. They also talked about the family environment at their school, the ways that the faculty works together, shares resources and ideas with each other, and supports the 650 children at their school, 90 percent of whom live below the poverty level.

Perhaps one answer to Seymour Sarason's question may be that there are more good city schools and teachers out there than we realize. We just need to find ways to better support their efforts with intelligent policymaking, like Senator Paul Wellstone's (2000) bill on high-stakes testing, and a renewed commitment to the Universal Declaration of Human Rights (United Nations 1948).

A Note on Educating Policymakers and the Public on Standardized Testing

Excellent sources are available for educating others about the problems with standardized testing, including Kohn (2000), McNeil (2000), Swope and Miner (2000), and Monty Neil's research and materials from Fairtest (www.fairtest.org). In addition to using these resources and ideas, readers might also consider some of the following reasons for opposing the use of high-stakes tests as the major measure of all student learning and potential.

1. **By supporting testing we are supporting frustration, alienation, and violence in schools across the country.** In a faculty meeting at Harrington, a teacher said that some of her students get so frustrated and angry when they are forced to take standardized tests that they may pick up their chair and throw it. Teachers in urban and suburban schools tell "test week" stories of students being frustrated to tears, children wandering the halls looking lost and afraid, and students looking dazed, discouraged, and "catatonic" for days after taking standardized tests. Testing is literally killing education. Children and youth across the United States are becoming less enthusiastic and engaged as learners, more turned off as students, less trusting of schools and teachers, and more disinterested and uncritical as readers. The sense of wonder, the curiosity and imagination, and the desire to question, experiment, and learn are in danger of extinction, particularly in our most underserved and overtested schools.

Just as students are increasingly stressed out, angry, and even violent due to mandated, high-stakes testing, some of the violence is turned inward, resulting in depression, alienation, and despair that makes students more susceptible to drugs, alcohol, and dropping or failing out of school. Some of the violence is turned outward against teachers and other students, exemplified at its worst in 1999 by the tragic massacres at Columbine High School in Littleton, Colorado.

In the midst of this, many excellent teachers are getting burned out and frustrated. Their knowledge and expertise as professionals are disrespected by the top-down testing mandates of noneducators who have no knowledge of the complexity of the teaching and learning processes, and no knowledge of the complexity of the classroom and school ecology.

The sorry U.S. history of testing parallels the U.S. eugenics movement in the 1920s (which Hitler took as a model), and the pre–World War II exclusion of millions of Eastern European Jews from immigration to the United States, based on culturally biased and invalid IQ scores (Gould 1998). Testing in the United States and abroad has contributed to the death and sterilization of over six million human beings, not to mention those whose dreams, opportunities, life chances, and self-worth have been irreparably destroyed.

2. By supporting the testing industry we are supporting a thief. Monty Neil from Fairtest estimates that well over a billion dollars is spent yearly on tests and preparation for the test materials that make publishing companies rich and education in the United States poor. But this sum pales in comparison with the dollar amount of teacher and student time that is wasted each year in preparing students for tests, administering the tests, grading and reporting on the tests, and meeting with parents, local authorities, and the general public to explain the results of the tests.

If there were some educational worth to all of this testing, it might seem somehow worth the astronomical costs. But, as we shall see in #3 below, there is not. Instead, testing (as well as preparation or "training" for testing) is time robbed from meaningful learning, which particularly disadvantages those who are in most need of more opportunities to learn.

Testing, and preparing for testing, has robbed teachers and students of the time and energy they need to devote to real learning. Testing steals precious time needed:

- for seeking their own questions
- for pursuing their own interests
- for following their own passions
- for listening to and communicating with one another
- for learning about both the individuality and the common humanity of one another
- for developing respect for one another's cultural heritages, languages, personal goals, strengths, and dreams
- for collaborating with one another to solve complex human problems that demand the best cooperative thinking of everyone—problems that are impossible to solve alone
- for developing community in and out of the classroom that is the antidote to fear, alienation, despair, anger, and violence

3. Asking the test score is the wrong question, because tests do not measure what we most value and need in twenty-first century learners. The new millennium requires critical and reflective thinking, creativity and imagination, motivation to continually relearn, flexibility in using multiple strategies, and the ability to work collaboratively on complex, individually unsolvable problems. One-right-answer, multiple choice, individually taken standardized tests cannot measure the kind of thinking and learning we most need and value. And preparing for these archaic, fossilized tests is an exercise in obsolescence (see #4 to follow).

Literacy research for well over forty years has confirmed what good teachers have always known: that language can only be evaluated in the context that gives it meaning. Yet despite a wealth of professional research knowledge, and despite the intuitive knowledge of excellent observant teachers, we are accepting invalid measures focused on disconnected and meaningless pieces of information. And we are allowing numerical results from invalid measures to masquerade as evaluation of successful student learning and good teaching.

Removing parts of reading and writing from their meaningful, functional, purposeful contexts for testing is as absurd as removing a heart or lung from the human body to test how well it is working. My favorite metaphor for this absurdity comes from Ken Goodman, who once said that any farmer can tell you that you don't find out how a carrot is growing by pulling it out of the ground. As in #1 above, this speaks to the very real danger in standardized and decontextualized testing of destroying that which you are supposedly trying to evaluate and improve.

4. By supporting standardized testing we are supporting the obsolescence of our system of education and endangering the survival of our democracy. In the complex world of today there are no simple one-right-answer solutions. Standardized tests are as obsolete as reliance on textbooks in the age of the Internet. Textbook sources are about as valuable as encyclopedia references for a credible research paper in the information age. Reference books and textbooks are very general and very limited sources of information, not to mention their sometimes narrow and shallow coverage of topics. Yet the same companies that produce the textbooks produce the tests that, coincidentally, are based on textbook information.

"Multiple-guess" formats, based on narrowly conceived and limited information, cannot come close to the kind of thinking and learning that is vital to the very survival of our democracy. And survival is not an exaggeration. It is no small coincidence that the literacy rate in Nazi Germany, as tested with standardized tests, and taught in literal textbook fashion, was the highest in the world (Haberman 1999).

We can teach narrow views very well this way. The alarming rise of hate groups across the United States (five hundred in 1999) attests to the success of this kind of narrowly conceived learning. What we cannot teach with textbooks and tests is human understanding, respect for the dignity and worth of all human beings, compassion for others, critical thinking about complex, multifaceted problems, and how to work collaboratively for the common good of our democracy.

A pluralistic democracy cannot survive unless its citizens can learn to understand, respect, and celebrate human differences, and unless they can develop a commitment to the common good. Presently we are well on our way to a more economically and racially divided society, with growing numbers of hate groups and a wider gap between the rich and the poor. We appear to be losing what Václav Havel of the Czech Republic has called the "soul" of democracy: the ability to tolerate diversity. And going beyond tolerance, we also lack respect and appreciation for the rich possibilities inherent in human diversity.

5. Standardized tests measure and reinforce standardized, conventional viewpoints and perspectives. Real critical thinking and learning demand multiple and competing points of view and openness to the perspectives of a wide variety of people. If we hope to go beyond the limitations of our current education system, if we hope to transcend shallow, visionless thinking, if we hope to rise above an inequitable status quo and more-of-the-same obsolescence, we will need better tools. We will need sources of information and evaluation measures that encourage critical thinking about such frequently excluded (from textbooks and tests) perspectives as:

- the Native American, in addition to the Columbus/explorer perspective, on "discovering" America
- the Japanese American stories of WWII internment camps in the U.S. and the aftereffects of Hiroshima
- present-day stories of U.S. Indian reservations along with the sad legacy of the trail of tears
- the resistance and heroism of African Americans in fighting slavery and segregation
- the stories of women—our founding mothers—resisting inequality and injustice along with the patriotism and rhetoric of our founding fathers
- the U.S. banning of the Spanish language in Puerto Rican schools along with the current bilingual education debates

Limiting ourselves to standardized textbooks and their accompanying standardized tests will be no help in the grand human endeavor before us of building a more equal, a more just, a more tolerant, and a more democratic society.

Developing an Ecologically Sound Approach

Successful learning is social, personal, integrative, transformative, and embedded within the larger ecology of the learner. It is interconnected and interdependent with the family, the school, the community, and the larger society. It is dependent upon the health, education, and welfare of the whole family.

Attempts to rip children out of their ecology, instead of strengthening and supporting their family and the community, have not been successful. The example of our early twentieth-century Indian schools, which removed Native American children from their families and communities to "civilize" them rather than supporting the traditions and values of their families and communities, suggests the failure of this approach. We begin the twenty-first century with continued severe poverty rates for Native Americans as well as high failure rates in school, increased drug and alcohol problems, and high adolescent suicide rates.

Our social policies continue to abuse and punish poor children and their families. And they disproportionately abuse and punish children of color, who are hardest hit by:

- the underresourced schools in their urban communities
- the underresourced hospitals and health clinics in their communities
- the absence of recreational, social, and artistic opportunities and activities
- the lack of good mental health facilities, social services, and other family supports vital to the health, education, and welfare of children in high-poverty communities
- the removal of social safety nets when child poverty and family crisis is increasing
- "zero tolerance" instead of teaching about and celebrating diversity
- the forced servitude of their mothers, who are no longer allowed to stay home with them
- the increased criminalization of their fathers and brothers who suffer from an unequal criminal justice system that disproportionately arrests and convicts African American and Latino men and boys

We cannot continue to imprison the fathers and brothers of millions of city children, and expect these children to do well in school. We cannot promote "zero tolerance" and arrest and imprison increasing numbers of adolescents of color, and expect them to learn successfully. The statistics on the racial imbalance in the criminal justice system belies the very name of justice (see Cole's *No Equal Justice* and Ayers' *A Kind and Just Parent*). And the absurdity of spending ninety-three thousand dollars per year to imprison a juvenile, while spending less than eight thousand dollars in the city school that failed them (Kozol 2000; Polakow 2000), cannot be matched anywhere else in the world.

An Ecological Approach to Successful City Teaching and Learning

Mapping the ecology of inequity from the entry point of preschool education, we can look at what it means in terms of standardized test scores when between 60 and 80 percent of the young children are denied preschool experiences. Kozol (2000) documented the reality in the South Bronx of only two out of ten preschoolers being admitted to the underfunded Head Start programs, and the further reality that two-thirds of the eligible preschoolers in this low-income community cannot be served by any program.

An important issue in U.S. preschool education is the high level of segregation by race and class. It has been said that the two most segregated times in the United States are Sunday morning in church and Monday morning in preschool classrooms. Separate, and quite different, preschool programs serve the children of the poor and the children of the affluent or middle-class.

In my visits to Head Start classrooms I have frequently seen much time devoted to such personal hygiene tasks as tooth brushing and hand washing, yet I have never seen this in a community nursery school in a suburban area or in a Montessori school. I often wondered about the comparative white middle-class benefit of more time spent with meaningful stories in preschool, along with access to good dental and medical services in the community.

Can we afford this? Again, we are presently spending sixty-four thousand dollars to incarcerate adults, the majority of whom are poor and undereducated. We are spending as much as ninety-three thousand dollars yearly to incarcerate children in juvenile detention centers, and the majority of these children have not had access to either a quality education or adequate medical, dental, and social services.

The United States has the highest incarceration rate in the world, which translates into a growing multibillion dollar business. It may be time to think about a new way to do business—one in which the cost in human pain and misery is not so high.

What would a reframing of the problem look like? I believe that we have the capacity to become more literate about both literacy and poverty. I believe that we have enough people of goodwill, enough people with a vision of the common good, enough people with a commitment to democracy and equality to reframe, reorganize, and reinvest in the business of developing the potentials of all of our citizens.

We can rediscover old ways and invent new ways to have more winners and fewer losers economically as well as educationally. This would be the beginning of an ecologically sound approach to successful city teaching and learning.

Epilogue

What are my biggest fears in writing this book? I fear that the enormously hard-won successes of these city teachers and schools will be treated as examples to hold up to all other urban schools, with the implication that it would be easy for them to do likewise. More specifically, I fear that inadequately informed policymakers will suggest that if these city teachers and schools in high-poverty areas can be successful, then the others can pull themselves up by their own bootstraps—when they have neither boots nor straps.

And similarly, I fear that readers will assume that success in urban schools is possible without vitally needed financial and educational resources, without supportive health and social services, without a tremendously committed and dedicated school staff, and without a knowledgeable, continually learning group of professionals in the school.

I also fear that readers will view the teachers and schools described in this book only through a narrow, quantitative, test-score lens, missing the long-term, deeply important, and vitally human aspects of learning that are being developed in urban youth—such as hope, compassion for and commitment to others, and a sense of their own heritage and potential.

And I fear that policymakers and the general public will not fully understand that over 55 percent of the variation in standardized test scores can be attributed to poverty factors, making evaluation based on such scores invalid, unjust, and abusive to poor children.

And perhaps most important, I fear that readers will think that success in city schools is possible without a larger societal commitment to equality and social justice; without the critical city, state, and national government leadership needed for long-term educational and social change; and without an informed citizenry that demands and supports both the change and the leadership.

These fears have paralyzed my writing and kept me from completing this book for the past four years. I do not want to contribute in any way to the continued disrespect of city teachers, schools, children, families, and communities. And my deepest fear is that somehow my writing will be used against the very people whose life work and commitment I most want to celebrate.

But I have watched the tragic societal neglect, disrespect, and abuse of urban children, families, teachers, and schools for too long. And I have watched the parallel rise in our prison population, which is now the highest in the world. Silence is not the answer. Nor is indifference.

One in every five children in the United States lives in poverty. This alone is unconscionable in the richest country in the world. But when one in every two children of color in the United States lives in poverty, we add another whole dimension to the problem. Silence, or being color-blind, is not the answer.

As mentioned in Chapter 7, Václav Havel, the leader of the Czech Republic, lamented that his country lacked the "soul" of democracy, which he went on to describe as tolerance and acceptance of diversity. As we look for models of democracy to share with the world, I believe that the teachers, parents, and other school and community leaders described in this book can show us great possibilities. They suggest what awaits us when we chose to do what Zinn (1994) calls us to do: "Live now as we think human beings should live, in defiance of all that is bad around us."

Howard Zinn reminds us that "to be hopeful in bad times is not just foolishly romantic. It is based on the fact that human history is a history not only of cruelty, but also of compassion, sacrifice, courage, and kindness."

> If we see only the worst, it destroys our capacity to do something. If we remember those times and places—and there are so many—where people have behaved magnificently, this gives us the energy to act, and at least the possibility of sending this spinning top of a world in a different direction.
>
> We don't have to engage in grand, heroic actions to participate in the process of change. Small acts, when multiplied by millions of people, can transform the world. (208)

But who am I to write this book?

(Journal, July 23, 1999)
> Sitting here on a peaceful dock at Deep Creek Lake, Maryland's "best kept secret," and rereading my fall 1996 and spring 1997 observation notebooks and fieldwork journals for

perhaps the fifth time this month, I continue to be amazed and in awe of the incredible work, the passionate commitment, the teaching skill, and the sheer artistry of the urban teachers, teacher leaders, and parents whom I have had the privilege of getting to know over the past four years. As I quietly relive my classroom, school, and community experiences, I say to myself, Who am I to even attempt to write about this? My feelings of inadequacy are overpowering, and I fear that my humble attempts to write about what I have seen will never do justice to those who, four years later, continue to amaze and inspire me. And every year since my return to college teaching, they have inspired my students as well.

But I also feel like an ungrateful taker, receiving the gifts that their lives are, not only to me and to my students, but to the hundreds of city children and families who are touched by them day after day. So it is with a feeling of gratitude and the desire to give back and to share their lives with others that I pursue the impossible goal of capturing some of their artistry and commitment — a goal that Gloria Ladson-Billings perfectly described as trying to catch lightning in a bottle.

This book has been a personal journey, but it has also been a collaborative one. It is written with, and in celebration of, the many city teachers, school leaders, parents, community members, and students that I have had the honor of getting to know in Philadelphia, Lancaster, and New York City. And it is written with the hope that their words, my observations, and the reflections of all of us as collaborators will inspire others to continue their work: to support their schools, communities, and families, and to renew a broad-based societal commitment to basic educational and economic human rights for all children and youth.

This is also a call to action to support the thousands of other urban public schools across the United States of America, and the millions of children and families that they represent. Collaboratively we can marshal the vitally needed, unprecedented commitment and support from policymakers and all citizens to make the new millennium one of equality and democracy, ensuring the sustainable welfare of our most vulnerable children and families.

As a wealthy and intelligent nation, we can do this, despite our periodic lapses into illiteracy about literacy and amnesia about child poverty. If the measure of a just society is the way that it treats its most vulnerable citizens, as a just and caring society, we *must* do this.

References

Allen, J. 1999. *Class Actions: Teaching for Social Justice in Elementary and Middle School.* New York: Teachers College Press.

Allen, J., B. Michalove, and B. Shockley. 1993. *Engaging Children: Community and Chaos in the Lives of Young Literacy Learners.* Portsmouth, NH: Heinemann.

Allington, R. 1995. *No Quick Fix: Rethinking Literacy Programs in America's Elementary Schools.* New York: Teachers College Press.

———. 1998. "Intelligent Teaching: Prevention and Intervention for Children at Risk for Failure in Reading." Presentation at the Fourth International Teaching for Intelligence Conference. April 25. New York City.

Apple, M., 1996. *Cultural Politics and Education.* New York: Teachers College Press.

———. 1999. *Official Knowledge: Democratic Education in a Conservative Age.* New York: Routledge.

Apple, M., and J. Beane. 1995. *Democratic Schools.* Alexandria, VA: Association for Supervision and Curriculum Development.

Armstrong, T. 1995. *The Myth of the A.D.D. Child.* New York: Dutton.

Ayers, W.1993. *To Teach: The Journey of a Teacher.* New York: Teachers College Press.

———. 1998. *A Kind and Just Parent: Children of the Juvenile Court.* Boston: Beacon Press.

Ayers, W., and P. Ford. 1996. *City Kids, City Teachers: Reports from the Front Row.* New York: New Press.

Barrs, M., S. Ellis, H. Tester, and A. Thomas. 1989. *The Primary Language Record.* Portsmouth, NH: Heinemann.

Bartoli, J. 1986. *Exploring the Process of Reading/Learning Disability Labeling: An Ecological Systems Approach.* Ann Arbor, MI: University Microfilms International.

———. 1995. *Unequal Opportunity: Learning to Read in the USA.* New York: Teachers College Press.

Bartoli, J., and M. Botel. 1988. *Reading/Learning Disabilities: An Ecological Approach.* New York: Teachers College Press.

Bateson, G. 1972. *Steps to an Ecology of Mind*. New York: Ballantine Books.

—————. 1979. *Mind and Nature: A Necessary Unity*. New York: Ballantine Books.

Beckmann, D., and A. Simon. 1999. *Grace at the Table: Ending Hunger in God's World*. New York: Paulist Press.

Blackburn, M. 1999. "Studying Privilege in a Middle School Gifted Class." In *Class Actions: Teaching for Social Justice in Elementary and Middle School*, edited by J. Allen, 72–83. New York: Teachers College Press.

Botel, M. 1999. Personal communication.

Bridges, L. 1995. *Assessment: Continuous Learning*. Los Angeles, CA: The Galef Institute.

Bronfenbrenner, U. 1979. *The Ecology of Human Development*. Cambridge, MA: Harvard University Press.

Carini, P. 1979. *The Art of Seeing and the Visibility of the Person*. Grand Forks: North Dakota Study Group on Evaluation, University of North Dakota.

—————. 1996. Personal communication. Philadelphia Teachers Learning Cooperative Workshop, Back Home Café at Project Hope, Philadelphia.

Children's Defense Fund. 2000. *The State of America's Children, 2000*. Washington, D.C: Children's Defense Fund.

Clay, M. 1993. *Reading Recovery: A Guidebook for Teachers in Training*. Portsmouth, NH: Heinemann.

—————. 1997. *Becoming Literate: The Construction of Inner Control*. Portsmouth, NH: Heinemann.

Cohen, M. 1980. *First Grade Takes a Test*. New York: Dell Publishing.

Cole, D. 1999. *No Equal Justice: Race and Class in the American Criminal Justice System*. New York: New Press.

Coles, G. 1987. *The Learning Mystique: A Critical Look at "Learning Disabilities."* New York: Pantheon.

—————. 1998. *Reading Lessons: The Debate over Literacy*. New York: Hill and Wang.

—————. 2000. *Misreading Reading: The Bad Science That Hurts Children*. Portsmouth, NH: Heinemann.

Cummins, J. 1989. *Empowering Minority Students*. Sacramento: California Association for Bilingual Education.

Darling-Hammond, L. 1992. "Achieving Our Goals: Superficial or Structured Reforms." *Phi Delta Kappan* 72 (4): 286–295.

Darling-Hammond, L., Ancess, J., and Falk, B. 1995. *Authentic Assessment in Action: Studies of Schools and Students at Work.* New York: Teachers College Press.

Darling-Hammond, L., and G. Sykes. 1999. *Teaching as the Learning Profession: Handbook of Policy and Practice.* San Francisco: Jossey-Bass.

Delpit, L. 1995. *Other People's Children: Cultural Conflict in the Classroom.* New York: New Press.

Derman-Sparks, L. 1989. *Anti-Bias Curriculum: Tools for Empowering Young Children.* Washington, D.C.: National Association for the Education of Young Children.

Derman-Sparks, L., and C. Phillips. 1997. *Teaching/Learning Anti-Racism.* New York: Teachers College Press.

Dewey, J. 1916. *Democracy and Education.* New York: Macmillan.

————. 1938. *Experience and Education.* New York: Macmillan.

Dyment, H. 1997. "The Yup'ik Encyclopedia of the Paul T. Albert Memorial School." *The Breadloaf Rural Teachers Network Magazine* (spring/summer): 6–7.

Fordham, S. 1990. "Racelessness as a Factor in Black Students' School Success." In *Facing Racism in Education,* edited by N. Hidalgo, C. McDowell, and E. Siddle. (Reprint Series # 21) Cambridge, MA: Harvard Educational Review.

Friere, P. 1981. *Education for Critical Consciousness.* New York: Continuum.

Friere, P., and D. Macedo. 1987. *Reading the Word and the World.* New York: Bergin and Garvey.

Funiciello, T. 1993. *Tyranny of Kindness.* New York: Atlantic Monthly Press.

Goodlad, J. 1987. *The Ecology of School Renewal.* Chicago: University of Chicago Press.

————. 2000. "Education and Democracy: Advancing the Agenda." *Phi Delta Kappan* 82: 86–89.

Goodman, K., and Y. Goodman. 1989. *The Whole Language Evaluation Book.* Portsmouth, NH: Heinemann.

Haberman, M. 1999. Speech delivered at the Kappa Delta Pi Convocation. November. Baltimore, MD.

————. 1999. *Star Principals: Serving Children in Poverty.* Indianapolis, IN: Kappa Delta Pi.

Haley, J. 1981. "Towards a Theory of Pathological Systems." In *Reflections on Therapy and Other Essays,* edited by J. Haley, 94–112. Washington, D.C.: Family Therapy Institute.

Halliday, M. 1978. *Language as Social Semiotic: The Social Interpretation of Language and Meaning*. Baltimore: University Park Press.

Hansen, J. 1987. *When Writers Read*. Portsmouth, NH: Heinemann.

————. 1998. *When Learners Evaluate*. Portsmouth, NH: Heinemann.

Heath, S. 1983. *Ways with Words: Language, Life and Work in Communities and Classrooms*. New York: Cambridge University Press.

Hobbs, N. 1978. "Families, Schools, and Communities: An Ecosystem for Children." *Teachers College Record* 79: 756–766.

Hoffman, L. 1981. *Foundations of Family Therapy*. New York: Basic Books.

Holdaway, D. 1979. *The Foundations of Literacy*. Portsmouth, NH: Heinemann.

Johnston, P. 1992. *Constructive Evaluation of Literate Activity*. White Plains, NY: Longman.

Kohn, A. 2000. *The Case Against Standardized Testing: Raising the Scores, Ruining the Schools*. Portsmouth, NH: Heinemann.

Kozol, J. 1992. *Savage Inequalities: Children in America's Schools*. New York: Harper Perennial.

————. 1996. *Amazing Grace: The Lives of Children and the Conscience of a Nation*. New York: Harper Perennial.

————. 2000. *Ordinary Resurrections*. New York: Crown.

Kuykendahl, C. 1992. *From Rage to Hope: Strategies for Reclaiming Black and Hispanic Students*. Bloomington, IN: National Education Services.

Ladson-Billings, G. 1994. *The Dreamkeepers: Successful Teachers of African American Children*. San Francisco: Jossey-Bass.

————. 2001. *Crossing Over to Canaan*. San Francisco: Jossey-Bass.

Lee, E., D. Menkart, and M. Okazawa-Rey, eds. 1998. *Beyond Heroes and Holidays: A Practical Guide to K–12 Anti-Racist, Multicultural Education and Staff Development*. Washington, D.C.: Network of Educators on the Americas.

Lieberman, A., and L. Miller. 1992. "Restructuring Schools: What Matters and What Works." *Phi Delta Kappan* 71 (10): 759–764.

————. 1999. *Teachers Transforming Their World and Their Work*. New York: Teachers College Press.

Lytle, S., and M. Botel. 1991. *The Pennsylvania Framework: Reading, Writing, and Talking Across the Curriculum*. Harrisburg: Pennsylvania Department of Education.

McDermott, R. 1987. "The Explanation of Minority School Failure, Again." *Anthropology and Education Quarterly* 18: 361–364.

McIntosh, P. 1989. "White Privilege: Unpacking the Invisible Knapsack." In *Beyond Heroes and Holidays*, edited by E. Lee et al. 1998. Washington, D.C.: Network of Educators on the Americas.

McNeil, L. 1986. *Contradictions of Control: School Structure and School Knowledge.* New York: Routledge.

—————. 2000. *Contradictions of School Reform: Educational Costs of Standardized Testing.* New York: Routledge.

Mehan, H. 1980. "The Competent Student." *Anthropology and Education Quarterly* 11: 131–152.

Meier, D. 1995. *The Power of Their Ideas: Lessons for America from a Small School in Harlem.* Portsmouth, NH: Heinemann.

Michalove, B. 1999. "Circling In: Examining Prejudice in History and in Ourselves." In *Class Actions: Teaching for Social Justice in Elementary and Middle School,* edited by J. Allen, 21–23. New York: Teachers College Press.

Minuchin, S. 1974. *Families and Family Therapy.* Cambridge, MA: Harvard University Press.

Moll, L. 1992. "Bilingual Classroom Studies and Community Analysis: Some Recent Trends." *Educational Researcher* 21 (2): 20–24.

Moll, L., D. Amanti, D. Neff, and N. Gonzales. 1992. "Funds of Knowledge for Teaching." *Theory into Practice* 31 (2): 132–141.

Napier, A., and C. Whitaker. 1978. *The Family Crucible.* New York: Harper and Row.

Palmer, S., M. Esolen, S. Rose, A. Fishman, and J. Bartoli. 1991. "I Haven't Anything to Say: Reflections of Self and Community in Collecting Oral Histories." In *International Annual of Oral History, 1990,* edited by R. Grele, 167–189. New York: Greenwood Press.

Phi Delta Kappa. 1997. "African American Males and the Criminal Justice System." October, Special Report.

Polakow, V. ed. 2000. *The Public Assault on America's Children: Poverty, Violence, and Juvenile Injustice.* New York: Teachers College Press.

Rist, R. 1972. "Student Social Class and Teacher Expectation: The Self-Fulfilling Prophesy in Ghetto Education." *Harvard Educational Review* 40: 411–451.

Rist, R., and J. Harrell. 1982. "Labeling the Learning Disabled Child: The Social Ecology of Educational Practice." *American Journal of Orthopsychiatry* 52: 146–160.

Rose, M. 1995. *Possible Lives: The Promise of Public Education in America.* New York: Houghton Mifflin.

Sarason, S. 1971. *The Culture of the School and the Problem of Change.* Boston: Allyn and Bacon.

————. 1990. *The Predictable Failure of Educational Reform.* San Francisco: Jossey-Bass.

————. 1996. *Revisiting "The Culture of the School and the Problem of Change."* New York: Teachers College Press.

————. 1999. *Teaching as a Performing Art.* New York: Teachers College Press.

————. 2000. Personal communication.

Schniedewind, N., and E. Davidson, eds. 1998. *Opening Minds to Equality: A Sourcebook of Learning Activities to Affirm Diversity and Promote Equity.* Boston: Allyn and Bacon.

Seccome, K. 1999. *So You Think I Drive a Cadillac? Welfare Recipients' Perspectives on the System and Its Reform.* Boston: Allyn and Bacon.

Shockley, B., B. Michalove, and J. Allen 1995. *Engaging Families.* Portsmouth, NH: Heinemann.

Sider, R. 2000. *Just Generosity: A New Vision for Overcoming Poverty in America.* Grand Rapids, MI: Baker Books.

Sizer, T. 1997. *Horace's School: Redesigning the American High School.* New York: Houghton Mifflin.

Skirtic, T. 1991. "The Special Education Paradox: Equity as the Way to Excellence." *Harvard Educational Review* 61: 148–194.

Smith, F. 1986. *Insult to Intelligence: The Bureaucratic Invasion of Our Classrooms.* Portsmouth, NH: Heinemann.

Southern Poverty Law Center. 1999. *Ten Ways to Fight Hate: A Community Response Guide.* Montgomery, AL: Southern Poverty Law Center.

Swope, K., and B. Miner, eds. 2000. *Failing Our Kids: Why the Testing Craze Won't Fix Our Schools.* Milwaukee, WI: Rethinking Schools, LTD.

Tatum, B. 1998. *Why Are All the Black Kids Sitting Together in the Cafeteria? And Other Conversations About Race.* New York: HarperCollins.

Taylor D. 1991. *Learning Denied.* Portsmouth, NH: Heinemann.

————. 1996. *Toxic Literacies: Exposing the Injustice of Bureaucratic Texts.* Portsmouth, NH: Heinemann.

Taylor, D., and C. Dorsey-Gaines. 1988. *Growing Up Literate: Learning from Inner-City Families.* Portsmouth, NH: Heinemann.

Teaching Tolerance Project. 1997. *Starting Small: Teaching Tolerance in Preschool and the Early Grades.* Montgomery, AL: Southern Poverty Law Center.

Thomas, L. 1992. *The Fragile Species.* New York: Scribner.

Torres, M. 1998. "Celebrations and Letters Home: Research as an Ongoing Conversation Among Students, Parents and Teacher." In *Students as Researchers of Culture and Language in Their Own Communities,* edited by A. Egan-Robertson and D. Bloome, 59–68. Cresskill, NJ: Hampton Press.

United Nations. 1948. *Universal Declaration of Human Rights.* New York: United Nations Department of Public Information.

Vygotsky, L. 1978. *Mind in Society.* Cambridge, MA: Harvard University Press.

Wellstone, P. 2000. "High Stakes Tests: A Harsh Agenda for America's Children." Speech at High Stakes Testing Conference. March. New York, Teachers College, Columbia University.

Zinn, H. 1994. *You Can't Be Neutral on a Moving Train.* Boston: Beacon Press.

Zucchino, D. 1997. *Myth of the Welfare Queen.* New York: Scribner.

Index